Borderline Personality Disorder

A Life-Changing Guide to Successfully Manage BPD, Protect Your Mental Health, and Cultivate Healthy Relationships

Lois Frost

Table of Contents

Introduction

I magine you are standing at the edge of a cliff, looking down into a chasm that seems impossibly deep. On one hand, you are paralyzed by fear, your heart racing, and your palms sweaty. On the other, you are captivated by the idea of diving headfirst into the unknown, craving the rush of adrenaline, the exhilaration of freedom. It is an intoxicating dance between terror and thrill, a tug-of-war between caution and impulsivity. This is not just a figment of the imagination, but a daily reality for some, a manifestation of a complex and often misunderstood condition – Borderline Personality Disorder (BPD).

Living with BPD can often feel like a constant battle within oneself. It is like being on an emotional rollercoaster that never stops, where feelings of joy can swiftly swing into intense sadness or anger. The unpredictability of emotions often leads to strained relationships and a profound sense of emptiness that seems to permeate every aspect of life.

Each day brings forth a new struggle; volatile emotions, the fear of abandonment, unstable relationships, and unclear or shifting self-image. The turmoil is exhausting, leaving one feeling as if they are constantly trying to navigate through a storm, lost and alone.

The challenges are further exacerbated by the lack of understanding and the misconceptions surrounding the disorder. It is a maelstrom of confusion and misconceptions, where empathy is replaced by judgment, and compassion is often overshadowed by fear.

Living with BPD is a daunting challenge, and the search for effective coping mechanisms can feel like a futile quest in an endless maze. The struggles are real, the pain is profound, and the need for an effective solution is ever more pressing.

Every labyrinth has an exit, every riddle has an answer, and every problem, however complex, carries within it the seeds of its own solution. For those living with the disorder, the key to the exit, the answer to the riddle, and the solution to the problem lie in understanding its nature, learning how to manage the symptoms, and implementing strategies to foster healthier relationships.

To get there, one does not need to traverse this challenging journey alone. Alongside you, as your guide, is a treasure trove of collective wisdom, distilled from the experiences of countless individuals who have navigated through similar struggles, as well as expert insights on managing BPD. The path forward does not require a drastic overhaul of your life overnight. Instead, it is a series of small, gradual changes, each one taking you a step closer to a life of balance, peace, and fulfillment.

There is no need for fear, and there is no room for despair. The change you seek resides within you, ready to be kindled into a beacon of hope, shining brightly through the storm. You have the power to change the narrative, rewrite the script of your life, and turn the page to a new chapter filled with understanding, healing, and growth.

Embarking on this journey of self-discovery and healing will unlock numerous benefits. The first and perhaps most important is the gift of understanding. With a deeper grasp of your own mind, the world around you begins to make more sense. The confusion that once shrouded your thoughts begins to lift, replaced by a newfound clarity that guides you in managing your emotions more effectively.

As understanding blooms, so does self-compassion. Acceptance of your feelings and struggles cultivates kindness toward yourself, fostering self-love and fostering resilience in the face of adversity. This self-compassion then extends outwards, helping to mend strained relationships and enabling you to build healthier ones.

Next, you will discover a set of practical, applicable strategies tailored to meet the unique challenges of living with the disorder. These tools will serve as your compass, guiding you through the tumultuous sea of volatile emotions, and leading you toward the shores of stability and peace.

Finally, embarking on this journey will inspire hope. Hope is a powerful motivator and a potent healer. It renews strength, instills courage, and ignites the spark of transformation. As you journey through these pages, you will find yourself infused with a renewed sense of purpose, a burning desire to reclaim your life from the grips of BPD, and the courage to stride confidently into a future filled with possibilities.

The insights and strategies shared in this book are not drawn from thin air but are the fruits of years of diligent exploration and research.

They are shaped by the stories of those who have lived and are living with **BPD**, their experiences molding the understanding of this complex disorder. Additionally, they are shaped by professionals working closely with these individuals, observing and learning from their journey.

This book serves as a bridge between these two worlds, the personal and the professional. It is an amalgamation of lived experiences and expert knowledge, combined to provide a holistic view of the disorder. It offers a unique perspective that is grounded in reality, free from academic jargon, and enriched by real stories of struggle and triumph.

However, this book is not a one-way street where I, as the author, provide you with all the answers. Instead, it is a dialogue where your lived experience is acknowledged, valued, and considered. The intention is to walk with you on your journey to understanding and managing the disorder, serving as your companion, your guide, and your ally. Together, we can navigate this path, and together, we can make a difference.

Journeys are never linear, particularly journeys of self-discovery and personal growth. There are peaks and valleys, moments of clarity, and periods of confusion. Yet, in every step, every stumble, and every stride, there lies the potential for learning, understanding, and growth.

This book aims to accompany you on such a journey, not by providing a rigid map to follow, but by offering a compass that can guide you through the terrain of BPD. It is about creating an internal shift, a ripple that starts small but eventually spreads, affecting your perceptions, responses, and interactions. This process can help mold a stronger, more resilient self, capable of weathering life's many storms.

The journey with this book is less about an endpoint and more about the continuous process of self-discovery, self-acceptance, and self-improvement. It is about empowering you to navigate your life's course with greater confidence, understanding, and compassion, both for yourself and for others.

Imagine a life where emotions no longer feel like a turbulent ocean, but more like a navigable river. Imagine relationships where misunderstandings are fewer, and connections run deeper. Imagine experiencing calm and control amid the chaos. This is the transformative power that understanding and managing the disorder can hold.

However, the longer one waits to start this journey, the longer these benefits remain just out of reach. There is an urgency not born out of fear, but from the promise of a more balanced, fulfilling life that awaits just beyond the horizon. Waiting will not make the journey easier or shorter. On the contrary, the delay only lengthens the shadow of the disorder, allowing it to cast deeper darkness over one's life.

Therefore, the best time to start is now. Not next week, not tomorrow, but today. With every moment spent in understanding, with each page turned, you are one step closer to that horizon, one step closer to reclaiming your life. This is not a journey you should embark on when time permits, but rather, one that demands to be embarked upon right now.

Walking the path with BPD, before finding the right tools and guidance, can feel like a trek through a dense forest without a map. The intensity and unpredictability of emotions often become an overbearing storm, difficult to weather. Relationships might feel like a dance on a tightrope, where a single misstep can lead to a devastating fall.

Living with the disorder can seem like an unending battle, where emotional turmoil is the relentless enemy. The constant fear of abandonment, the tendency to swing from one emotional extreme to another, can create a profound sense of helplessness. It is as if you are trapped in a maze, running in circles, seeking a way out, but only encountering dead ends.

Striving for a stable emotional life and meaningful relationships can appear a Herculean task, especially when you feel misunderstood, stigmatized, or alone in your struggle. The journey to understanding and managing BPD can seem like a long, winding road filled with obstacles and setbacks.

But acknowledging this struggle is the first step toward transformation. Recognizing the need for change and seeking the right help can be the beacon that guides you out of the darkness.

Despite the complexities, there is always room for hope, resilience, and recovery.

You might be seated comfortably right now, book in hand, seeking answers or perhaps you are in the throes of emotional turmoil looking for a lifeline. This journey you are about to embark upon is not just about reading another book. It is about walking a path toward understanding, acceptance, and eventually, profound transformation. This journey is about reclaiming your life, your relationships, and your self-esteem. You have weathered the storm of emotional extremes, now it is time for a season of healing. The resilience that has brought you this far will serve as your guide. Embrace this opportunity to transform your challenges into stepping stones, turning your struggles into strength.

Remember, every chapter you traverse in this book is a step toward empowerment. Each page turned, a stride toward self-awareness. And every word absorbed is an invitation to reimagine your life, not as a person living with BPD but as an individual thriving despite it. This is a voyage of self-discovery. It is not about eradicating the disorder from your life, but about understanding it, managing it, and using it as a tool to shape your own unique narrative. You have the power to redefine your life, to paint it with vibrant strokes of courage, resilience, and hope. As you move forward, remember, you are not alone. Many have walked this path before you and many will follow. This journey is about connection and growth. It is about understanding yourself in a deeper, more compassionate way. This journey is for you. Now, let us begin.

Chapter 1:
Exploring What Lies Beneath

Unpacking Stigma and Challenging Misunderstandings

P icture this: A woman, Sara, is late for work. Her car would not start, and her phone battery is dead. Once she finally makes it to work, her boss reprimands her, and she is left feeling upset and misunderstood. It seems like a bad day, right? But now, imagine experiencing the same intensity of emotional upheaval, not just because of an unfortunate sequence of events, but from everyday life's usual ups and downs. Welcome to a glimpse into the world of someone with borderline personality disorder.

It is crucial to begin with a fact: This disorder is one of the most stigmatized and misunderstood mental health disorders. Many misconceptions exist, painting individuals with BPD as manipulative, attention-seeking, or even dangerous. Such stereotypes stem from a lack of understanding and are, unfortunately, further fueled by inaccurate depictions in the media and popular culture.

But the reality is profoundly different, and we need to debunk these misconceptions to foster empathy and support for those living with the disorder. BPD is not a choice. It is a complex mental health condition that affects how individuals perceive themselves, others, and the world around them, causing severe emotional instability. Labeling these individuals with derogatory terms does not just fail to encapsulate their struggle, but it also leads to further isolation and discourages them from seeking help.

Here is the truth: Those living with BPD are not "attention-seeking." Their emotional reactions may seem exaggerated or out of proportion because they experience emotions more intensely and for more extended periods than others. What might be a small trigger for some can lead to a tidal wave of emotions for someone with the disorder. It is not a cry for attention; it is a cry for help and understanding.

Also, individuals with BPD are not inherently manipulative. Yes, they may exhibit behaviors that seem manipulative, such as self-harming or threatening suicide. However, these actions are often desperate attempts to manage their overwhelming emotions or prevent perceived abandonment. They are not calculated strategies to manipulate others.

Moreover, people with the disorder are not dangerous by default. While some individuals with BPD may have episodes of anger or engage in risky behaviors, it is essential to understand that not everyone exhibits these traits. Furthermore, when such behaviors do occur, they are usually self-destructive rather than directed toward others.

Another misconception we need to dispel is that BPD is untreatable. Yes, it is a chronic condition, but it is also highly treatable. Many individuals with the disorder experience significant improvement over time, with appropriate therapy and support.

As we progress, let us keep in mind that we are not just discussing a clinical condition; we are talking about individuals. They are mothers, fathers, daughters, sons, friends, and lovers struggling to navigate their lives in the turbulent sea of their intense emotions. They deserve understanding, empathy, and support as they traverse their journey, not stigmatization and judgment.

In dispelling these myths and misconceptions, we are not just enriching our understanding of BPD. We are opening doors to empathy, fostering environments for support, and most importantly, validating the experiences of those living with this condition. It is a significant first step in going beyond the surface of BPD. And as we go deeper, you will see that there is more to the disorder than meets the eye.

The Distorted Reflection of Reality in the Media

Imagine tuning into your favorite television show, the anticipation building as the plot unfolds, only to be confronted with a character that is meant to represent a person with BPD. However, the representation is woefully inaccurate; the character is volatile, manipulative, and seemingly incurable. You are left with a disheartening portrayal, one that perpetuates stereotypes and intensifies the stigma associated with the disorder. Sadly, this is a reality for many people living with this condition.

The media, with its broad reach and influence, holds a potent role in shaping public perceptions of mental health issues. Regrettably, portrayals of BPD often miss the mark, painting the condition as synonymous with chaos and destruction. Such characterizations are not only unfair but damaging, contributing to a climate of misunderstanding and prejudice against individuals living with the disorder.

But why does this happen? To answer that, let us delve into the mechanics of storytelling. A compelling narrative often leans on conflict and high stakes, and the complex emotions associated with the disorder can be twisted into a sensationalized spectacle. However, this approach overlooks the breadth and depth of the human experience behind the diagnosis. The sensationalization of BPD does more harm than good, sowing seeds of misunderstanding that can lead to misdiagnosis, mistreatment, and further stigmatization.

To illustrate this, consider the popular film "Girl, Interrupted." While the film attempts to shine a light on the struggles of mental illness, the main character, diagnosed with BPD, is depicted as manipulative, unstable, and, ultimately, beyond help. This portrayal, while dramatic and engaging, fails to capture the entirety of the BPD experience, with its challenges, strengths, and potential for recovery.

Further exacerbating the issue, these skewed representations of BPD often fail to address the underlying causes of the disorder, such as genetic factors, environmental influences, or traumatic experiences. By omitting this crucial information, the media narrative feeds into a damaging myth: Those with BPD are simply "problematic," rather than individuals navigating a complex mental health condition.

Now, imagine an alternate reality, one where media portrayals of BPD are accurate, compassionate, and comprehensive. A world where characters with the disorder are depicted not as destructive forces but as complex individuals capable of growth and healing. Such portrayals could play a significant role in fostering a more understanding and empathetic society.

The media can – and should – do better. By striving for accuracy in their portrayals of BPD, they can move from being part of the problem to part of the solution. And there are signs of positive change. Some contemporary series and films have begun to explore the disorder with more sensitivity and depth, providing nuanced portrayals that challenge stereotypes and offer hope.

However, this shift must go beyond merely "getting it right." Media creators have a responsibility to consult mental health professionals and people with lived experience of BPD during their creation process. This collaborative approach could ensure a more accurate and empathetic depiction of the disorder, encouraging greater understanding and acceptance in the viewing audience.

In the next section, we will delve further into the complex inner world of individuals with BPD, revealing the struggles, triumphs, and human experiences that lay behind the labels and misconceptions. Together, we can work toward a more compassionate understanding of the disorder, challenging the distortions that have cast a long shadow over this condition.

Revealing the Inner Turmoil of BPD

As we peer into the world of someone living with BPD, it is essential to approach with an open heart and mind, ready to understand their struggles. For a moment, let us imagine ourselves on a roller coaster – a towering, imposing structure. As we climb into the seat, the safety bar lowers with a decisive clunk. And then, we are off. Up, up, up, the coaster ascends, only to hurtle down at breakneck speed. Our hearts leap into our throats, stomachs knot, and breaths hitch. This is thrilling for a brief stint at an amusement park, but imagine this wild ride every day, relentlessly, with no means of getting off. Welcome to the emotional world of a person living with BPD.

People with the disorder often find themselves on an emotional roller coaster, characterized by intense feelings that can change rapidly. Their emotions are not just more potent; they are also more volatile. For many of us, if we had a heated argument with a friend, we might stew about it for an hour or so, then move on. However, for someone with BPD, that same disagreement might trigger a cascade of powerful emotions that last for days, coloring their entire perception of the relationship.

Now, this emotional turbulence is not a choice; it is not a sign of weakness or a character flaw. It is a component of BPD, a consequence of how the brain responds to emotional stimuli. Remember how we discussed the misconceptions about the disorder in the first section? One of the biggest is the idea that these individuals are overly dramatic or attention-seeking. In reality, they are grappling with genuinely overwhelming emotions, to the point where they might feel controlled by them.

The emotional world of someone with BPD could be likened to a house of mirrors. The mirrors magnify and distort emotions, causing relatively minor incidents to reflect as monumental crises. But these mirrors also twist self-perception. Many people with the disorder suffer from chronic feelings of emptiness, a sense of being fundamentally flawed or worthless. They might feel like a puzzle with missing pieces, trying to present a complete picture to the world while internally grappling with a sense of incompleteness.

Simultaneously, it is important to note that individuals with BPD are not always in the throes of emotional turmoil. They have periods of relative calm, too. However, even during these times, they may live in fear of when the next emotional storm might strike, perpetuating a cycle of anxiety.

Having a glimpse into these internal struggles is not meant to evoke pity, but understanding. It is to empathize with their battles and validate their experiences. Their reality, while often arduous, is just as genuine as ours. They are not asking for our judgment or offering an invitation to "fix" them. They need our compassion, our patience, and, most importantly, our willingness to stand by them, even when their emotions become tempestuous. In the next section, we will explore the hidden strengths often found in individuals with BPD, reinforcing the idea that, despite their struggles, they possess resilience and unique attributes that are truly admirable.

Unveiling BPD's Hidden Strengths

Life is a palette of colors. For some, it may seem like a consistent spectrum, while for others, it is a constantly evolving canvas. For individuals with BPD, their canvas might at times appear overwhelmingly intense or painfully desolate. But what if amid the turmoil and struggle, there lie hidden strengths, unseen capabilities, waiting to be unveiled?

One of the most remarkable strengths of individuals with BPD is their resilience. Imagine you are aboard a small boat in a stormy sea, tossed around by wave after wave. You would have to have an incredible degree of resilience to navigate your way to calmer waters. Those with the disorder live this metaphor daily, navigating emotional storms that would leave many feeling lost. In surviving these internal maelstroms, individuals with BPD develop a resilience that can be harnessed and transformed into a potent force for personal growth and change.

If you are reading this and you are living with BPD, take a moment to recognize your own resilience. You have survived your worst days. You have weathered storms that others cannot even comprehend. Your resilience is not just a survival tool; it is a testament to your strength. How can you use this strength to your advantage? The first step is to acknowledge it. Celebrate it. Recognize that every time you have been knocked down and got back up, you have been flexing your resilience.

Another hidden strength in many with BPD is empathy. This heightened emotional sensitivity can often lead to an intense understanding of others' feelings. You may find you are the person friends come to when they need support or understanding, simply because you "get it" on a level that others do not. This deep empathy can be nurtured and transformed into a powerful tool for connection, understanding, and even advocacy.

However, this strength comes with a responsibility. To be able to use your empathy constructively, you need to be able to manage your emotional boundaries effectively, so you are not overwhelmed by the emotions of others. Start by noticing when your empathetic nature kicks in. Are there particular situations where you feel the emotions of others more intensely? By becoming aware of these situations, you can better prepare for them and manage your response.

Lastly, there is a vibrant stream of creativity that runs deep in many people with BPD. The intense emotions and vivid internal experiences can fuel an artistic and creative drive. Writing, painting, music, drama – these are not just forms of expression, but also powerful therapeutic tools for managing and understanding your emotional world.

To tap into your creativity, start by exploring different forms of artistic expression. You might find solace in painting, find release in music, or discover self-understanding through writing. Do not be concerned about creating something "good" or "impressive." This is about the process, not the product. This is about using creativity as a way to explore, express, and manage your emotional landscape.

In conclusion, BPD can undoubtedly be a challenging journey. But remember, every journey has its rewards. And for those living with the disorder, resilience, empathy, and creativity are treasures to be discovered and honed. As we move forward, let us keep these strengths in mind, learn to celebrate them, and find practical ways to use them to our advantage. Remember, amid the struggle, there is strength. You are much more than your disorder. Your journey is unique, and your strengths are your own. Recognize them. Nurture them. Celebrate them. And most importantly, use them.

Chapter 2:
Navigating the Turbulent Journey of Emotions

Swinging Between Emotional Highs and Lows

I magine sitting on a pendulum, swinging from one extreme to another with no control over its course. One moment, you are at the height of exhilaration, basking in the sunlit glow of joy. The next, you are hurtling toward the cold, dark abyss of despair. This is the daily reality for someone with BPD, living with emotional dysregulation – a core feature of the disorder. But what exactly is emotional dysregulation, and how does it affect the lives of individuals with this condition? Let us explore.

Emotional dysregulation is the inability to manage intense emotional responses. While everyone experiences ups and downs, individuals with BPD experience these fluctuations with such intensity that they are often likened to emotional third-degree burns. Simple, everyday interactions or events might trigger an overwhelming flood of emotions that feel impossible to control.

Imagine you are running late for an appointment. It is a common occurrence for many of us and may cause a twinge of anxiety or frustration. But for someone with BPD, this can be a catalyst for a surge of intense shame, anger, or even despair. It is not just the intensity, but also the rapid change between emotions that can be disorienting and exhausting.

Living with such emotional turbulence can be like navigating through a relentless storm. It affects various aspects of life, including relationships, work, and self-esteem. The emotional intensity can lead to strained relationships, as loved ones may struggle to understand the rapid mood swings. The inability to maintain emotional stability can impact professional life, affecting job performance and career growth. The constant self-doubt and emotional turmoil can also wear down a person's self-esteem over time.

So, what can be done about it? How can someone with the disorder manage this emotional whirlwind? First, it is important to understand that emotional dysregulation is not a personal failure or weakness. It is a part of the disorder, and recognizing this can help reduce the stigma and self-blame often associated with these intense emotions.

Next, identifying triggers can be incredibly helpful. Is it a specific situation, like running late or feeling criticized, that causes the emotional surge? Or perhaps it is a certain time of day or physical sensation? While it is not always possible to avoid triggers completely, being aware of them can offer a sense of control and prepare one for managing the emotional response.

Finally, know that help is available. BPD is a complex disorder, but it is not untreatable. Many therapeutic approaches specifically target emotional dysregulation, equipping individuals with the skills to manage their emotions more effectively. In the following sections, we will delve deeper into these therapies and explore practical strategies for coping with emotional dysregulation.

In the face of such emotional turmoil, it is crucial to remember that you are not alone. Countless individuals are on this same journey, finding ways to manage their emotions and live fulfilling lives despite the challenges. The pendulum may swing wide and wild, but you hold the power to slow its course and, ultimately, find balance. Let us embark on this journey of understanding and managing emotional dysregulation in BPD together.

Sparkling the Catalysts of Mood Fluctuations

Have you ever lit a candle? The tiny spark from a match or a lighter meets the wax-soaked wick and in an instant, a flame bursts forth, dancing and flickering with warmth. Now, imagine your emotions as that flame. Certain events, people, words, or even thoughts are your matches. These are your triggers, and they hold the power to ignite intense mood swings.

Understanding these triggers is not merely about highlighting what "lights your emotional candle." It is a voyage of self-discovery, allowing you to explore the depths of your emotions and arming you with the knowledge to navigate through the emotional rollercoaster that is BPD.

Firstly, let us acknowledge this: Your triggers are personal. They are unique to your experiences, thoughts, and perceptions. For some, a trigger could be a comment from a loved one, an unexpected change in plans, or feeling ignored in a social setting. Others might find themselves in emotional turmoil due to a significant date, an anniversary of a traumatic event, or an encounter that reminds them of past distress.

It might be easy to fall into the trap of judging yourself for what triggers you or how intensely you react. Let us pause for a moment here. Remember, your feelings are valid. Your emotions are not "over-the-top" or "unnecessary." They are a response to your triggers, a mirror reflecting your past experiences and existing coping mechanisms.

Once we acknowledge this, we can start taking steps toward managing these triggers. It begins with self-awareness. Keep a journal of instances where you find your mood swinging disproportionately. Document the circumstances, your thoughts, and how you responded emotionally. This exercise is not to critique yourself but to detect patterns and recurring themes, which could be your triggers.

But what next? Here comes the crucial part – planning. Imagine walking through a familiar path in the dark. You know there is a pit somewhere along the way. Would you stumble into it or navigate around it, knowing it is there? Identifying your triggers is knowing where the "pit" is. Now you can strategize how to maneuver around it.

This strategy could involve setting boundaries. For instance, if certain conversations trigger you, it is okay to express your discomfort and steer the discussion toward safer shores.

Sometimes, avoiding a trigger might not be possible. In such situations, a coping mechanism comes into play. This could be a grounding technique, like focusing on your breath or your surroundings. You can also try "emotional surfing." Envision your emotions as waves. Instead of fighting against them, allow them to wash over you. Accept their presence but remind yourself that, just like a wave, this too will recede.

However, the most crucial advice I can offer is this: Seek professional help. Psychologists and therapists are equipped to provide you with a personalized set of tools to identify, understand, and manage your triggers effectively. They can also help you to unpack the underlying experiences that have led to these triggers, facilitating deeper healing.

In the upcoming section, we will dig deeper into understanding the intense emotions that characterize BPD. As we walk this path, remember that this journey is yours. Each step, no matter how small, is a stride toward greater self-understanding and emotional balance. So let us move forward, one step at a time.

Understanding the Profound Emotions of BPD

Have you ever found yourself swept away in a torrent of emotions, akin to a leaf caught in a raging river? One minute you are cruising atop the water's surface, basking in the warmth of the sun, and the next you are tumbling under the weight of the rushing currents, gasping for air. If you have experienced these intense and rapidly fluctuating emotional states, it can feel as if you are living through a perpetual storm, never certain when the next gust of wind will sweep you off your feet. This is often the reality for individuals living with BPD.

Emotions for those with BPD are not just emotions; they are vivid, potent, and consuming experiences that can dictate the course of a day or the trajectory of a life. They are not always negative – they can be intense joy, profound love, and immense hope. However, they can also be deep despair, burning anger, or paralyzing fear. This emotional intensity can bring with it a heightened sense of empathy, a connection to the world around you that others might not experience. Yet, these emotions, as strong as they are, are not your masters. They are part of you, but they do not define you.

To understand these intense emotions and navigate life with BPD, you first need to understand the nature of emotions. Emotions are not right or wrong, good or bad. They are a part of our human experience. They are responses to our environment, our thoughts, and our beliefs. However, when these emotions become too intense, they can feel overwhelming and can lead to impulsive actions or reactions.

A key to managing these intense emotions is recognizing them for what they are – responses. Let us consider a practical strategy for achieving this, a technique known as "emotional labeling." This simple, yet effective, tool involves recognizing an emotional response, naming it, and allowing yourself to experience it without judgment.

For instance, suppose you are suddenly filled with an inexplicable sense of dread. Instead of being swept away in the tide of fear, pause. Acknowledge the emotion. Say to yourself, "I am feeling scared." Do not try to push the emotion away or criticize yourself for feeling it. Simply acknowledge it, label it, and let it be. With time, this can help decrease the intensity of your emotional reactions and give you a sense of control over your emotional landscape.

It is also crucial to remember that emotions are temporary states. They ebb and flow, much like the tides of the ocean. Even the most intense emotions will pass with time. When you are caught in the throes of a powerful emotion, it can feel all-encompassing, as if it will last forever. But remember, "This too shall pass." Use this phrase as a mantra, a reminder that you have weathered these emotional storms before and you will do so again.

Understanding and managing your intense emotions can feel like a monumental task. But remember, you are not alone in this journey. Reach out to trusted friends, family, or mental health professionals who can provide guidance, support, and reassurance. Know that with each wave you weather, you are becoming stronger, more resilient, and more capable of navigating your emotional seas.

Navigating intense emotions is just one part of the journey with BPD. In the following section, we will explore some therapeutic approaches and coping strategies to help achieve emotional stability. Through these methods, you will gather the tools necessary to build your ship, ready to brave any storm.

Striving for Emotional Balance

Seeking emotional stability while grappling with BPD may seem like an uphill battle. But remember, even the highest mountains can be climbed with the right tools and strategies. So, let us explore some of these practical solutions for nurturing emotional balance.

For a start, you are not alone on this journey. Many have navigated these tumultuous waters before, and there is much wisdom to glean from their experiences. Accepting help in the form of therapy can make a world of difference. Cognitive behavioral therapy (CBT) and dialectical behavior therapy (DBT) have proven particularly effective in managing emotional dysregulation in BPD. Therapists using these methods provide tools to identify and modify thought patterns that lead to destructive emotions and behavior. With time and consistent practice, this can help you gain control over your emotional responses.

In the realm of self-help strategies, mindfulness emerges as a significant aid. Mindfulness, the practice of living in the present moment without judgment, can be a soothing balm for emotional turmoil. It brings your attention away from past regrets or future anxieties and grounds you in the now. You could start with a simple five-minute mindfulness meditation each day, focusing on your breath or the sensations in your body. Over time, you might notice a certain tranquility seeping into your daily life, a tranquility that helps stabilize emotions.

On this note, mindfulness should not be restricted to meditation. It is a skill that you can weave into your everyday activities. For instance, mindful eating, where you savor each bite and truly experience the flavors, can transform a routine activity into an act of emotional grounding.

Exercise, too, can be a potent tool in your emotional stability toolkit. Regular physical activity, whether it is a brisk walk in the park or an intense workout, can help release pent-up emotions and reduce feelings of anxiety and depression. It has been scientifically proven to boost your mood and improve your overall emotional health.

Lastly, a technique often used in DBT called "opposite action," can help you counter intense emotions. Here is how it works: When you experience a strong, unhelpful emotion, you consciously choose to act in a way opposite to what that emotion is compelling you to do. So, if anger is pushing you to lash out, you consciously choose to respond with kindness. If fear urges you to isolate yourself, you decide to reach out to a friend instead. By acting in direct opposition to your unhelpful emotions, you begin to break their control over you.

While these strategies may be helpful, remember, it is okay if you do not get it perfect every time. Be gentle with yourself. You are learning and growing, and that in itself is a success. Healing is not linear, and every step, no matter how small, is a step forward.

Seeking emotional stability when living with BPD is a journey filled with self-discovery, resilience, and personal growth. As you move forward, may your steps be steady and your spirit unbroken.

Chapter 3:
Emancipating From the Chains of Self-Shame

Confronting the Harsh Reflection of Self-Shame

As we embark on this journey through the labyrinth of BPD, we encounter a cruel adversary that is often deeply ingrained within the psyche of those battling this condition. This adversary goes by the name of self-shame.

If you have ever felt like an imposter, believing that you are not good enough, or perhaps constantly comparing yourself to others and finding yourself lacking, you have met self-shame. It is an insidious force, slipping in unnoticed, quietly sowing seeds of doubt and self-criticism. It paints a distorted image in the mirror of our minds, whispering tales of inadequacy and unworthiness.

For individuals with BPD, self-shame can be amplified, much like an echo in a canyon, distorting their self-perception and intensifying feelings of worthlessness and self-loathing.

Let us consider for a moment the origin of this self-shame. It is often rooted in childhood experiences, where messages from parents, teachers, and peers, both explicit and subtle, might have suggested that we are "not enough." Over time, these experiences can become internalized, morphing into a critical inner voice that continues to echo these negative messages long after the original sources have fallen silent.

The damaging effects of self-shame on mental health are immense. It erodes self-esteem, fuels anxiety, contributes to depression, and can even trigger self-harming behaviors. When we are ensnared in the throes of self-shame, it feels as though we are trapped in a vicious cycle, where every failure or perceived rejection serves as "proof" of our unworthiness.

But it is important to remember that self-shame is not an accurate reflection of who we are. It is a distorted lens, a warped mirror that only shows us our faults, real or imagined, while blinding us to our strengths and accomplishments.

Now, how do we break free from this cruel mirror of self-shaming?

The first step is to recognize it. Listen to your inner dialogue. What are you telling yourself? Is it a voice of support and understanding or one of harsh criticism and blame? Are you constantly berating yourself for every mistake, or do you accept that you are human and that humans are allowed to err?

Recognizing the voice of self-shame is an essential first step, but it is not an easy one. It requires courage to face the harsh words we tell ourselves, and it demands honesty to admit that we have been our own worst critic.

But as you stand before this cruel mirror, know that you have the power to shatter it. You can challenge the voice of self-shame and replace it with one of self-compassion and understanding. As we move forward, remember that you are not alone on this journey. Many have stood before the same mirror, and many have found their way through to a more compassionate self-understanding.

This journey might seem daunting, but the first step has already been taken. You have faced the mirror and recognized self-shame. This is the beginning of a transformative journey, a journey of breaking free from the shackles of self-shame and stepping into a more compassionate relationship with yourself.

Embracing Compassion Instead of Judgment

Imagine for a moment, the comforting warmth of a gentle embrace after a long, tiring day. How soothing is that embrace, how it seems to instantly ease all the tensions? Now, what if you could wrap yourself in such an embrace, not just physically, but emotionally and mentally? This is what choosing compassion over judgment does. It envelops you in a kind, understanding hold that validates your pain and struggles instead of criticizing or berating them.

Choosing self-compassion can feel foreign, especially if you have spent years being your harshest critic. But remember, breaking self-shame's shackles is not an overnight process; it takes time, patience, and consistent practice. So, let us explore some practical ways to choose compassion over judgment.

To start, you need to catch yourself in the act of self-judgment. Is there a particular time of day when the self-doubt creeps in? Is it after a perceived failure or setback? When you learn to recognize these patterns, you can start challenging them. If it helps, keep a journal to track these instances, write down what you were doing, how you were feeling, and the thoughts that arose.

Next, try to reframe your self-judgment. For instance, instead of saying, "I messed up again, I am useless," you could say, "I made a mistake, but it does not define me. Everyone makes mistakes, and it is okay." Practice saying these kinder, compassionate statements to yourself, out loud if possible.

A critical aspect of choosing compassion over judgment is acknowledging and validating your feelings. Many people with BPD try to suppress their feelings, especially the unpleasant ones, and criticize themselves for having them in the first place. But remember, it is okay to feel what you feel. You are human, and emotions, both good and bad, are a part of the human experience. Next time you feel overwhelmed, try saying to yourself, "It is okay. It is natural to feel this way. I am here for myself."

Meditation can be a powerful tool in your journey toward self-compassion. Try a loving-kindness meditation, where you send messages of love and kindness to yourself and others. It might feel strange or even uncomfortable at first, but over time, it can significantly shift your mindset from judgment to compassion.

Lastly, it is essential to remember that nobody is perfect, including you. Perfection is an unattainable standard that only feeds self-judgment and shame. Embrace your imperfections, and see them as unique parts of your story, your character, that make you who you are.

Choosing compassion over judgment is not an easy switch. There will be days when you will feel like you have made no progress. But remember, every step, no matter how small, is a step forward. And as you continue to practice self-compassion, over time, it will become less of a practice and more of a way of living.

Conquering the Inner Critic

Have you ever felt imprisoned by your negative thoughts? The endless cycle of self-criticism and judgment feels like an insurmountable mountain. You are not alone. Many people with BPD experience this harsh inner critic, a voice that incessantly picks apart every mistake, every perceived flaw. It is a voice that can be deafening and debilitating. But it is also a voice that can be quieted and eventually silenced.

Overcoming self-judgment begins with awareness. Start paying attention to the way you talk to yourself. What kind of language do you use? Is it kind and encouraging, or harsh and critical? If a friend were to speak to you in the same way, would you find it acceptable? Often, we treat ourselves far worse than we would allow others to treat us. Understanding this discrepancy is the first step in breaking the chains of self-judgment.

Next, practice challenging these negative thoughts. When that inner critic pipes up, confront it with logic. If it tells you that you are worthless because you made a mistake, remind yourself that everyone makes mistakes. Mistakes are growth opportunities, not proof of inadequacy. If the voice insists that you are unlovable, remember the people in your life who love and care for you. These are your weapons in the battle against self-judgment.

It is also important to create a nurturing inner voice. Visualize a kind, caring figure. This could be someone you know, a mentor, or even a fictional character. When you are wrestling with self-judgment, imagine what this nurturing figure would say to you. By developing this comforting inner voice, you create a counterweight to the harshness of the critic.

Keep in mind that overcoming self-judgment is not about suppressing negative thoughts or forcing positivity. It is about meeting those thoughts with understanding and challenging them with the truth. It is about shifting from a mindset of criticism to one of compassion.

Practicing self-compassion means treating yourself with the same kindness and understanding you would offer a friend. It is about acknowledging that you are human, that you make mistakes, and that is okay. In moments of struggle, it might help to say to yourself, "This is really hard for me right now. How can I comfort and care for myself at this moment?"

In the journey of overcoming self-judgment, there will be setbacks. The critical voice might get louder during times of stress or when you are feeling vulnerable. It is important to approach these moments with gentleness. Remember, you are not your thoughts. You can observe them, challenge them, and choose not to engage with them.

Let us pause here to reflect. Ask yourself, how can you challenge your inner critic today? What nurturing messages can you give yourself?

Remember, this is a process, not a destination. With patience and persistence, the grip of self-judgment will gradually loosen, making way for self-compassion to heal your soul. As you close this chapter and move on to the next, carry this newfound understanding of self-compassion and mindfulness, for they will be your companions in the journey ahead.

Fostering a Gentle and Supportive Inner Voice

In the voyage of healing and overcoming self-shame, one of the most critical steps you can take is to nurture kinder inner dialogue. Much like cultivating a garden, the process involves patience, consistent effort, and a deep understanding of what you are striving to grow. But rest assured, with time, the results can be astonishing and life-transforming.

Let us begin by understanding what inner dialogue means. It is that subtle voice within us, our self-talk, shaping our perceptions, actions, and reactions. We all have this voice, but in the case of BPD, it tends to be harsh, self-critical, and unforgiving. For many, it feels as if they are constantly at war with themselves.

Imagine for a moment that your thoughts are like radio waves, always present and influencing you. What station are you tuned into? The station that tells you that you are unworthy, that you are a burden, that you are less than perfect? Or the one that gently reminds you that it is okay to stumble, that growth is a process, and that every effort you make, however small, is worthwhile?

The first step toward building a kinder inner dialogue is becoming aware of the current narrative. Spend some time each day noting down your thoughts. Do not judge them; simply observe. Are they primarily negative? Do you often criticize or blame yourself? Awareness is the first step toward transformation.

Once you have identified the patterns of your self-talk, begin gently to challenge these narratives. Ask yourself, "Is this thought helpful or harmful? Is it based on evidence or assumption?" Self-compassion is not about denying reality; it is about viewing it through a more balanced lens.

But how do you replace these negative thought patterns with positive ones? One practical way to do this is by using affirmations. Affirmations are positive statements that you repeatedly say to yourself, which can help to override damaging thought patterns. Some examples include: "I am doing my best, and that is enough," "I deserve kindness and understanding," or "I am a work in progress."

This is not to suggest that you can think your way out of BPD or any mental health condition, rather it is to underline the influence of self-talk in our lives. It is not about ignoring negative emotions or experiences, but rather treating yourself with the same kindness, empathy, and understanding you would extend to a friend.

Visualization is another powerful tool. Imagine your mind as a garden. The negative thoughts are weeds, and the positive thoughts are flowers. To help your garden flourish, you must water the flowers and pluck out the weeds. This metaphor can be an excellent guide as you begin to consciously shape your inner dialogue.

Mindfulness and cognitive-behavioral techniques can also be useful in this process. Mindfulness helps you become more aware of your thought patterns, while cognitive-behavioral techniques help in challenging and changing harmful narratives. You may wish to seek professional guidance to learn and practice these techniques.

Building a kinder inner dialogue is a journey, one that requires patience and persistence. Do not be disheartened if old thought patterns resurface; it is part of the process. Remember, every step, no matter how small, is progress. Your words have power, especially the ones you say to yourself. With time, effort, and patience, you can cultivate an inner dialogue that supports your healing and growth.

The journey to breaking the shackles of self-shame does not end here, though. In the next part of this journey, we will unravel another facet of BPD, the often-misunderstood trait of impulsivity, and how mindfulness can serve as a powerful tool in balancing it.

Chapter 4:
Impulsivity and Mindfulness in Balance

Exploring Impulsivity in BPD

I mpulsivity is a word that often carries negative connotations. But what is it, really? When we hear "impulsivity," we might think of a sudden, unplanned trip to the mall, or an unexpected, last-minute decision to adopt a pet. While these acts could be considered impulsive, they are also relatively harmless. However, when it comes to BPD, impulsivity takes on a much more consequential nature.

At its core, impulsivity is a lack of restraint, a seemingly uncontrollable urge to act on one's immediate feelings or desires, without considering the potential outcomes. For those living with BPD, this impulsivity can infiltrate every aspect of their lives, from interpersonal relationships to financial decisions, job choices, and more. It is not merely a casual, spur-of-the-moment purchase; it is a constant battle against sudden urges that can lead to life-altering consequences.

Have you ever felt a strong surge of emotion that made you want to act instantly, with little regard for the repercussions? It is a familiar feeling to those with BPD. Imagine that sensation is amplified and occurring repeatedly, and you begin to understand the intensity and frequency of these impulses for those with the disorder.

This impulsivity arises from various sources. A key cause is the emotional volatility that characterizes BPD. Intense emotions can drive hasty actions. When feelings of anger, sadness, or elation become overwhelming, acting impulsively can seem like the only way to alleviate or express those feelings.

Another root cause is the pervasive sense of emptiness that many with BPD experience. The emptiness can feel so unbearable that they may engage in impulsive behaviors to fill the void, even if momentarily. It is a frantic search for something – anything – to make them feel alive, connected, or real. This might manifest as impulsive spending, substance abuse, risky sexual behaviors, or binge eating.

Impulsivity in BPD also extends to relationships. Rapid changes in feelings toward others can result in impulsive actions such as sudden breakups, intense declarations of love, or aggressive confrontations. These actions are often driven by the fear of abandonment, a hallmark of BPD, and can result in a self-fulfilling prophecy as relationships become strained and often break down.

What is crucial to remember is that this impulsivity is not a choice. It is a symptom of a deeper struggle – a desperate attempt to cope with overwhelming emotions or to fill an internal void. Understanding this can lead to empathy for those struggling with BPD, and it can also serve as a stepping stone for those living with the disorder to start addressing their impulsivity.

The question then becomes, how can you manage these impulses? How can you slow down the rapid-fire decision-making and take a step back before acting? If you or a loved one is living with BPD, what strategies can be employed to gain better control over these potentially destructive behaviors? These questions will guide our journey in the following sections. Together, we will uncover effective strategies to curb impulsive actions, learn how to cultivate mindfulness and encourage deliberate decision-making. While the journey may be challenging, remember that every step you take is a step toward reclaiming your life from the grip of impulsivity.

This journey does not need to be taken alone. With professional help, self-help strategies, and the support of loved ones, managing impulsivity in BPD is indeed possible. Your journey begins with understanding, continues with action, and blossoms into a more stable, fulfilling life. As we embark on this voyage, know that there is hope for change, hope for control, and hope for a brighter future.

Impulsivity and Its Domino Effect

Imagine for a moment that you are standing on top of a hill, overlooking an expansive valley. In your hand, you hold a single domino piece. This domino, seemingly insignificant, represents an impulsive decision. With a small flick, you release the domino down the hill. It swiftly tumbles, knocking into another, then another, setting off a chain reaction. Such is the impact of impulsivity in BPD.

The downhill tumble of the domino, or your impulsive action, may seem harmless at first, perhaps even exhilarating, providing immediate gratification or relief from an intense emotional state. However, each subsequent domino it strikes represents unforeseen consequences. These could range from damaged relationships, precarious financial conditions, compromised health, or an emotional backlash of guilt and regret.

Understanding the domino effect of impulsivity is paramount in addressing it effectively. Real-life examples abound, shedding light on the consequential chain reaction. Consider a spontaneous decision to go on a shopping spree when you are feeling low. It might provide instant gratification and a brief respite from distress. However, the subsequent dominoes that fall could include maxed-out credit cards, financial stress, and regret over unnecessary purchases.

Similarly, impulsively quitting a job due to a disagreement with a coworker may feel empowering at the moment, but the dominoes that tumble after may represent financial insecurity, potential loss of reputation, and the stress of job hunting.

Think of an argument with a loved one that escalates quickly due to an impulsive response. The dominoes that follow might include hurt feelings, potential relationship strains, and subsequent emotional turmoil for all parties involved.

Emphasizing the domino effect of impulsive behavior is not meant to provoke guilt or self-blame. Instead, it serves as an illumination tool. It highlights that an impulsive decision is not a standalone event; it sets off a series of consequences that can extend well beyond the initial action.

You might be thinking, "Well, that sounds daunting. Is every decision I make going to set off a series of disastrous events?" Not at all. Recognizing the potential domino effect of impulsivity does not mean that every choice leads to a negative outcome. However, it underscores the importance of pause, of taking a moment to consider the possible impacts before setting the first domino in motion.

It is about empowerment through awareness, building your understanding so that you can harness your decision-making process. With this awareness, it becomes possible to replace impulsive reactions with thoughtful responses. It is an opportunity to stop the dominos before they start cascading, preventing the potential fallout.

While the domino effect can seem overwhelming, remember that understanding is the first step toward change. And even the longest chain of dominos starts with a single piece. In the next part of this chapter, we will delve into practical strategies to manage impulsivity, allowing you to gain more control over that first domino. You are not alone on this journey, and together, we can navigate this hill.

Tactics for Managing Impulsive Behavior

First and foremost, remember that you are not alone in your battle against impulsivity. Many people, not just those with BPD, wrestle with impulsive behavior. The key is not to suppress this behavior but to manage it, much like a sailboat captain harnesses the wind, rather than fights against it.

One particularly effective strategy for curbing impulsive actions is what we will call the "Pause and Reflect" technique. When an impulsive urge arises, take a moment to pause, step back, and consider the potential consequences of the action you are about to take. This pause acts as a circuit breaker, interrupting the impulsive response and providing space for reflection. Over time, you will find that this pause becomes second nature, allowing you to make more considered decisions.

Another powerful tool at your disposal is "Distraction and Diversion." Find healthy and engaging activities that can serve as a "go-to" distraction when you feel the pull of impulsive action. This could be anything from reading a book, taking a walk, playing a musical instrument, or even completing a puzzle. The purpose here is not to ignore or run away from your feelings but rather to divert your attention until the urge subsides.

Just as we need to exercise our bodies to keep them fit, our impulse control muscles also need regular workouts. Regular practice of mindfulness exercises can help you manage impulsivity. One simple exercise is "Mindful Breathing." Find a quiet place, close your eyes, and focus all your attention on your breathing. Notice the sensation of air entering and leaving your body. If your mind wanders, gently bring your focus back to your breath. This practice will enhance your ability to stay focused and calm under pressure.

Let us not forget the importance of maintaining a healthy lifestyle. Regular physical activity, a balanced diet, and adequate sleep contribute to overall well-being and are critical in managing impulsivity. Regular exercise, in particular, has been shown to help reduce impulsive behavior by increasing the brain's production of endorphins, neurotransmitters that promote feelings of well-being and satisfaction.

Lastly, do not hesitate to seek help when you need it. Therapy, particularly cognitive behavioral therapy (CBT) and dialectical behavior therapy (DBT), can be beneficial. These therapies help you understand your triggers, develop effective coping strategies, and improve your emotional regulation skills. Remember, it is not a sign of weakness to seek help, but a testament to your strength and determination to manage your impulsivity.

It is essential to remind ourselves that change does not happen overnight. Progress may sometimes feel slow, but every step you take toward managing your impulsivity is a victory. It is not about being perfect; it is about making consistent efforts to better manage your impulses. Celebrate each success, no matter how small, and do not be too hard on yourself when things do not go as planned.

The journey to manage impulsivity may be challenging, but with patience, perseverance, and the right strategies, you can take control of your actions and steer your life in the direction you wish. The upcoming section will further delve into cultivating mindfulness and patience as an aid to this process. Remember, you are the captain of your ship, and you have the power to navigate your journey with grace and resilience.

How to Develop Mindfulness and Patience

So, how do we navigate through the forest of impulsivity, taking one step at a time? We will need a trusty compass to guide us, and in our journey, that compass is mindfulness. Mindfulness, at its core, is a practice of paying full attention to the present moment, embracing it without judgment, and releasing the grip of our preoccupations, worries, and anxieties. By cultivating mindfulness, we are training ourselves to pause, listen, and choose our response rather than being swept away by impulsive tides.

The beauty of mindfulness lies in its simplicity. Yet, do not be fooled by its seeming simplicity; it has profound implications for managing impulsivity. It allows us to understand our thoughts and emotions as they are, without getting tangled in them. It is like watching clouds in the sky, observing them as they float by without attempting to change their direction or pace.

As a person living with BPD, your mind might feel like a battlefield, with thoughts and emotions battling for dominance. Mindfulness allows you to become the observer of this battle, rather than a participant. The more you can observe without judgment, the more likely you are to break the chains of impulsive actions.

To cultivate mindfulness, you can start with simple, daily practices. Mindful breathing, for instance, is a technique that involves focusing on your breath's rhythm and acknowledging the thoughts that come without becoming immersed in them. Try this: Close your eyes, take a deep breath, hold it for a moment, and exhale slowly. As you breathe in and out, allow your attention to stay with the breath. If your mind wanders, gently bring it back to the breath. Practice this for a few minutes each day and gradually increase the duration.

Along with mindfulness, patience is a key ally in managing impulsivity. If mindfulness is our compass, then patience is our walking stick, helping us to steady ourselves when the path gets rough. Patience allows us to pause and assess the situation, consider the potential consequences of our actions, and choose a response that serves our best interests.

How do we cultivate patience in the face of pulsating, pressing emotions? Begin with the understanding that patience is not about suppressing or denying your feelings. It is about acknowledging them and giving them space, but not allowing them to take the driver's seat.

One practical strategy for fostering patience is to implement the "Pause Principle." When you feel the wave of impulse starting to build, instead of acting on it, take a moment to pause. It might be a few seconds or a few minutes – whatever time you need to let the wave peak and start to subside. During this pause, engage in a grounding technique like mindful breathing or sensory grounding, which involves focusing on your five senses to anchor yourself in the present.

Through consistent practice of mindfulness and patience, you can begin to build a buffer zone around your emotions. This buffer zone gives you room to move, think, and choose. It is like taming a wild river into a gently flowing stream. It is not about denying the river's power but about guiding it in a direction that serves you.

Remember, these practices are not about achieving perfection. There will be times when you slip and when impulsivity gets the upper hand. That is okay. Every moment is a new opportunity to practice, learn, and grow. And with each mindful step, you are carving your path toward a life of greater peace and control. Your journey of mastering impulsivity, powered by mindfulness and patience, is a testament to your resilience. Celebrate it, for each moment of awareness is a victory in itself.

Through the lens of mindfulness, we see that impulsivity is not an unassailable fortress, but a mountain that can be climbed, one mindful step at a time. On the next climb, we will explore how to navigate the whirlwinds of intense relationships.

Chapter 5:
Managing Intense Relationships with BPD

A Journey Through the Whirlwinds of Passion

S tep into the shoes of an artist about to splash his vibrant emotions onto a blank canvas, a dancer swaying to the rhythm of her heart, or a poet narrating the saga of a heart on fire. Imagine feeling emotions not just as gentle breezes but as whirlwinds of passion. This is often the reality for individuals with BPD navigating relationships. The depth and intensity of their emotions can be as beautiful and awe-inspiring as a raw, untamed force of nature. However, as with any storm, it can also be overwhelming, both for the individual and for the people close to them.

Let us start by understanding why relationships can be particularly intense for individuals with BPD. The answer lies in their deeply empathetic nature. They can often feel other people's emotions as if they were their own. Now, imagine the effect this heightened empathy could have on intimate relationships. It is like experiencing the world in high definition, where all emotions are magnified.

For instance, love for them is not just a soft, warm glow; it is a burning, all-consuming flame. Happiness is not just a gentle ripple; it is a euphoric high. In contrast, fear is not just a minor worry; it is a bone-chilling terror. Pain is not just an ache; it is an agonizing torment. Anger is not just an irritation; it is a roaring, seething rage.

They experience emotions at a volume most people might never understand.

What does this intensity mean for their relationships? Let us take the example of romantic relationships, where emotional stakes are high. They may fall in love quickly and passionately; driven by an intense emotional connection they feel with their partner. Every interaction, every shared laughter, every intimate moment feels profound, exhilarating. It is like living a sweeping epic love story every day.

However, these heightened emotions are not always rosy. They can also lead to intense fear and vulnerability. Fear that their loved one will not reciprocate their strong feelings. Fear of being seen as too needy, too emotional, too much. Vulnerability because letting someone into their world means exposing them to the raw, unfiltered intensity of their emotions.

This intense emotional whirlwind can make relationships with individuals with BPD both deeply rewarding and immensely challenging. Rewarding because they can offer an unparalleled depth of love, empathy, and connection. Challenging because their partners might find the intensity of their emotions overwhelming.

Understanding these emotional whirlwinds is the first step in navigating relationships with individuals with BPD. The key is not to pathologize or judge them for their emotional intensity but to empathize with their unique emotional experience. It is about acknowledging that their emotions, while intense, are very real and very valid.

Remember, understanding does not imply an obligation to endure harmful behaviors. It is about realizing that what might seem like "overreactions" are their emotional reality. It is about helping them not drown in their emotional whirlwinds and learning how to dance in the rain together.

Confronting the Fear of Abandonment

An understanding tone can be especially valuable when addressing the deeply ingrained fear of abandonment that often lies at the heart of BPD. This fear is not an occasional nuisance; it can be a terrifying, ever-present specter, shadowing even the most routine interactions.

Imagine an invisible rubber band connecting you to the people you care about most. You desire closeness, and when you have it, you bask in its comforting warmth. But any real or perceived sign of separation pulls that band to its limit, triggering panic and desperation. That is the closest many of us can come to understanding the dread of abandonment experienced by someone with BPD.

Does this sound familiar to you? If so, do not lose hope. Acknowledging your fear is the first step toward managing it, and there are concrete strategies you can adopt.

First, practice mindfulness. When feelings of panic or desperation arise, rather than being swept away by the emotional storm, ground yourself in the present moment. Observe your surroundings, pay attention to your breath, and feel the chair beneath you or the ground under your feet. You may find that by anchoring yourself in the physical world, the emotional whirlwind becomes less overwhelming.

Second, try to shift your focus. When you are terrified of someone leaving, your attention naturally hones in on every potential sign of their withdrawal. However, this hyper-vigilance can distort your perception and fuel your fear. Try to consciously shift your focus onto other aspects of your life or relationship. What are your shared joys? What are your strengths? Taking a more balanced perspective can help reduce the power of your fear.

A third strategy involves the challenging task of reframing your thoughts. Instead of telling yourself, "If this person leaves me, I will not survive," try to remind yourself that you have value and resilience independent of this relationship. It is a long process, and it is perfectly okay if you do not believe it right away. The goal is to gradually change your self-narrative so that fear of abandonment does not define your self-worth or dictate your interactions.

Last but not least, consider professional help. If your fear of abandonment is overwhelming and deeply rooted, it might be beneficial to seek the assistance of a therapist who specializes in BPD or related issues. They can provide you with tailored strategies and therapies like CBT or DBT, which have shown promising results in managing such fears.

Embracing these strategies will not erase your fear overnight. The journey may be long and fraught with challenges. Yet, each step you take toward understanding and managing your fear of abandonment is a testament to your strength and resilience. Remember, progress is not linear, and each person's journey is unique. But by gradually integrating these strategies into your daily life, you are laying the groundwork for healthier relationships and a stronger, more self-assured you.

Creating and Maintaining Healthy Relationship Boundaries

How does one create a sense of safe space within relationships, especially when those relationships are continuously under the strain of intense emotions? As we navigate this intricate journey of understanding and managing BPD, one crucial aspect to explore is the establishment of healthy relationship boundaries.

Firstly, it is essential to recognize that boundaries are not barricades, but rather guidelines that define a relationship. They allow for the growth of mutual respect, provide a sense of security, and establish a shared understanding of what is acceptable within the relationship.

Now, let us explore how one can establish these healthy boundaries.

Understand Your Needs: Your needs and desires matter. Acknowledging this is the first step in setting boundaries. What do you need in terms of personal space, emotional support, or respect? Identifying these needs can guide you in defining your boundaries.

Communicate Effectively: Effective communication is key. It is important to express your needs assertively, yet respectfully. Your feelings are valid, and conveying them sincerely can help others understand your point of view.

Define Consequences: Be clear about the consequences if your boundaries are violated. This is not about punishing others, but about safeguarding your emotional health. It is crucial to follow through with these consequences, or else your boundaries will hold no weight.

Practice Consistency: Be consistent with maintaining your boundaries. This may require repetition and resilience, especially if others are used to overstepping your boundaries. But remember, consistency is key to making these boundaries effective.

Bear in mind, setting boundaries is not a one-time event but a dynamic process that needs continuous work and adaptability. It is also equally essential to respect the boundaries of others, creating an environment of reciprocal respect and understanding.

Of course, this process is not easy, especially when dealing with BPD's intensity. It might sometimes feel as if you are walking a tightrope, trying to balance your needs with your fear of abandonment or rejection. But remember, your needs and feelings matter just as much as anyone else's. Establishing boundaries might seem challenging initially, but in the long run, it brings stability, clarity, and strength to your relationships.

To those reading this who are supporting someone with BPD, understand that your role is not to fix them, but to support them. Setting healthy boundaries does not mean distancing yourself, but rather defining the relationship in a way that respects and honors both parties involved.

As we journey forward, let us remember that change takes time, patience, and persistence. Healthy relationships are a two-way street, and just as you strive to understand and empathize with a loved one with BPD, they too are learning to understand and manage their condition. Your compassion and support, combined with clear boundaries, can provide a safe space that can help nourish and sustain the relationship.

In the next part, we will further explore the realm of relationships, this time delving into the role of secure attachments in the healing process. Remember, every step you take, no matter how small, is a step toward progress.

Exploring Attachment, Relationships, and the Healing Process

We have explored the intensity and the passion of relationships involving individuals with BPD, discussed the all-consuming fear of abandonment, and delved into the necessity of establishing healthy boundaries. Now, let us step further into the journey of healing by looking at the significant role of secure attachments in recovery, accompanied by tangible strategies to foster such connections.

Imagine that the psyche of a person with BPD is a ship adrift on turbulent seas. The fear of abandonment is like a storm, always on the horizon, threatening to capsize the vessel. The intense emotions, the volatility, and the struggles with self-image are all powerful waves that threaten to throw the ship off course. Amid this tumult, the idea of a secure attachment is like a sturdy anchor providing stability amid the chaos.

The theory of attachment, first proposed by psychiatrist and psychoanalyst John Bowlby, explains that secure attachments in early life lay the foundation for healthy emotional development and relationships. Individuals with BPD often have experienced disrupted or insecure attachments in their past, leading to instability in their emotional world.

Creating secure attachments as an adult, however, can be a potent healing force. These attachments do not necessarily need to be romantic. They can be close friendships, relationships with therapists, or bonds with supportive community members. The key factor is a sense of trust, consistency, and emotional safety within the relationship.

Building these types of connections involves vulnerability, something that may be particularly challenging for someone with BPD. It requires expressing emotions honestly and trusting that the other person will respond with understanding and compassion. It requires the belief that it is okay to lean on someone else for emotional support and that this will not lead to abandonment or rejection.

Practically speaking, how does one cultivate these secure attachments?

Firstly, awareness is the stepping stone to change. Understand the patterns that may be preventing you from forming secure relationships. Are you pushing people away for fear they will abandon you? Are you excessively clinging to relationships, scared to give the other person space? Recognizing these patterns is the first step toward altering them.

Next, communication is crucial. Start expressing your needs and fears to the people you trust. It may feel uncomfortable at first, but remember that it is okay to need others and ask for help. Let your loved ones know when you are feeling vulnerable or scared of abandonment. This honesty not only helps to reinforce your bonds but also allows those around you to understand and support you better.

Thirdly, try to build a consistent and predictable structure in your relationships. This could mean establishing regular check-ins with your friends or scheduling consistent appointments with your therapist. Stability and predictability can help reduce the fear of abandonment and the intense emotional swings associated with unpredictability.

Finally, patience is paramount. Building secure attachments will not happen overnight, especially if you have been navigating the stormy seas for a long time. Allow yourself grace, understanding that it is a journey filled with progress and setbacks. Celebrate your achievements, however small they may seem. Every step taken is a step closer to calm waters and toward healing.

Remember, you are not alone on this voyage. By creating and nurturing secure attachments, you are setting the stage for a more balanced emotional life and paving the way for a brighter, healthier future.

Chapter 6:
Choosing Resilience in the Face of Glass Shards

Self-Destructive Patterns to Look Out For

As if emerging from the morning fog, let us gently bring our attention to a challenging but crucial aspect of the BPD journey – self-destructive patterns. This might seem like a daunting prospect. Yet, it is essential to remember that recognizing these patterns is not an end but a new beginning, the first critical step toward change and recovery.

Imagine standing at the edge of a vast forest, the woodlands of your mind, where familiar paths are etched deep into the earth, trodden by years of habit. Some of these paths lead to places of self-destruction – perhaps self-isolation, substance abuse, or unhealthy relationships. Recognizing these well-worn paths is the initial step on the journey of transformation.

Borderline personality disorder often co-occurs with certain risky behaviors, a direct result of the intense emotions, feelings of emptiness, or fear of abandonment that hallmark this disorder. These behaviors might include reckless driving, binge eating, substance misuse, or engaging in unsafe sexual activity. For some, self-harm might become a way to cope with unbearable emotions. Others may oscillate between idealizing and devaluing people, causing tumultuous relationships.

So, how do you recognize these self-destructive patterns? Start by developing an observer's perspective of your life. Imagine watching a movie about your daily routines, relationships, and responses to stress. Notice any repeated actions that lead to negative consequences for your physical or mental well-being.

Next, consider your emotional responses. Do certain actions or decisions often follow feelings of emptiness, abandonment, or self-loathing? Can you trace a direct line between these intense emotions and self-destructive behavior? Connecting the dots this way helps to identify triggers and the behaviors that follow.

Journaling can be a helpful tool in this process. Dedicate a few moments each day to reflect and jot down any behaviors you have noticed and the emotions that preceded them. Over time, patterns might emerge from these pages, guiding your understanding and providing a roadmap to change.

Remember, the goal here is not to judge or shame yourself for these behaviors, but to gently acknowledge their existence. You are not your behaviors, and recognizing these patterns is a sign of strength, not a fault. It is about gaining clarity, understanding the "why" behind your actions to forge a new path toward healing.

Recognizing self-destructive patterns also includes acknowledging their role in your life. Paradoxically, these patterns often evolve as a means of survival, a way to cope with the emotional chaos that BPD can bring. They are misguided attempts to protect yourself, to control or numb overpowering emotions. Understanding this can help you approach these patterns with compassion instead of criticism.

Recognition is a potent agent of change. It is the first flicker of dawn, promising a new day. Now, having recognized these patterns, you might wonder, "What next?" In the following sections, we will be exploring strategies to address these patterns, transforming them from stumbling blocks into stepping stones. This recognition is the start of your resilience story, an initial step in turning shards of glass into stepping stones toward recovery.

Tackling Self-Harm and Suicidal Ideation

Self-harm and suicidal ideation are painfully raw realities that we need to address with great sensitivity when it comes to BPD. But before we examine the depths of these issues, let me emphasize one thing: No matter how dark the night is, there is always a glimmer of dawn waiting for you. This is not a hollow promise; this is the testament of thousands who have trodden the path before you, finding their way out of this labyrinth of despair.

In the silence of self-harm and suicidal thoughts, you are not alone. Statistics show that up to 80% of people with BPD have suicidal thoughts, and about 75% have self-harmed at some point. This is not to add to your burden but to let you know that many have felt this weight and still found the strength to rise, and so can you.

Why do these dark thoughts occur? They are often a way of coping with intense emotional pain, an escape hatch from feelings that seem unmanageable. Yet, they are temporary relief and bring about more harm than healing. Remember, self-harm is not the answer, nor is it a solution to the chaos within.

For those who are worried about a loved one, understand that talking about self-harm or suicidal ideation does not increase the risk. It is actually beneficial, a release valve for pent-up pain. Let us break the taboo.

When someone opens up to you about their struggles, how do you respond? With patience, empathy, and openness. There is a profound power in lending an empathetic ear. Do not try to offer solutions immediately, simply listen. Your presence can be a sanctuary for someone battling their own thoughts.

To those wrestling with these thoughts, I want you to know that seeking help is not a sign of weakness but an act of courage. Reaching out to someone you trust – be it a friend, family member, or a mental health professional – can be your first step toward healing. You do not have to carry this burden alone. There are helplines available around the clock, ready to help you navigate through your darkest hours.

Yet, it is important to build long-term strategies to manage this pain. This involves developing a safety plan – a roadmap that helps guide you when your thoughts take a dark turn. Your safety plan could include recognizing your personal warning signs, listing coping mechanisms that have worked for you in the past, detailing whom to reach out to when in crisis, and establishing professional contacts for emergencies.

At this point, I cannot help but stress the importance of professional help. Therapies like CBT, DBT, and Eye Movement Desensitization and Reprocessing (EMDR) have proven to be incredibly beneficial. They equip you with strategies to handle emotional turbulence, helping you step away from self-harm as a coping mechanism.

But remember, the most crucial element of this journey is you. Your commitment to fighting, your resilience to rise from setbacks, and your determination to weave a narrative of hope with threads of despair. You matter. You are more than your pain. Your life has value beyond what you can perceive in the depths of your despair. Always hold onto that truth.

In the next section, we will explore effective techniques for crisis intervention, focusing on the essential role of professional assistance in diffusing critical situations.

Effective Techniques for Crisis Intervention

Let us begin a conversation about crisis intervention, a topic that can feel intimidating, yet it is crucial for individuals with BPD and their loved ones. Please remember, there is always help available, and no one is expected to face these trials alone. Let us explore some key strategies and tools to manage crises.

One critical technique for crisis intervention is to create a crisis plan. This is a guide for individuals with BPD and their loved ones to know what steps to take when a crisis occurs. A crisis plan may include recognizing warning signs of a crisis, listing calming strategies, identifying support networks, and contact information for mental health professionals or helplines.

Recognizing the warning signs is a pivotal step. Early signs might include intense feelings of distress, sudden mood swings, feelings of hopelessness, or even dissociative episodes. Keep in mind that these signs will vary for different individuals. The important aspect is understanding personal triggers and signs that a crisis may be emerging.

Once the warning signs are apparent, calming strategies are essential to employ. These strategies should be personalized to the individual's needs. For some, this might involve deep-breathing exercises or guided meditation. For others, distraction techniques such as listening to music, painting, or going for a walk might be helpful. The primary objective here is to divert the overwhelming thoughts or emotions that could lead to crisis escalation.

The support network plays a significant role during a crisis. This network often includes family, friends, therapists, or even support groups. It is beneficial to list these contacts in the crisis plan. Remember, it is okay to lean on others during tough times. Reaching out for support is not a sign of weakness but rather a testament to resilience and strength.

Lastly, but equally important, is the inclusion of contact information for mental health professionals or helplines. These resources provide immediate assistance during a crisis. It is beneficial to familiarize oneself with these resources in non-crisis times to reduce panic or confusion during actual crises.

This plan, however, does not substitute professional help. If an individual is in immediate danger or contemplating self-harm, immediate medical attention should be sought. Crisis hotlines are available 24/7 and can provide immediate support and assistance.

Crisis intervention is also not a one-time solution but an ongoing process. Regular therapy can equip individuals with skills to handle intense emotions and can provide a platform for exploring and addressing root causes that contribute to crises. Therapies such as CBT and DBT are particularly effective in helping individuals with BPD manage their emotions and reduce the occurrence of crises.

In conclusion, preparing for a crisis is not about expecting the worst; it is about arming oneself with the knowledge and tools to effectively manage if such a situation arises. By creating a crisis plan and seeking professional help, individuals with BPD can empower themselves to navigate through these challenging situations. Ultimately, it is about taking one day at a time, acknowledging that it is okay to ask for help, and believing in one's ability to overcome adversities.

Inspiring Stories of Hope and Recovery

Sometimes, when life seems to be a perpetual storm, the best thing we can do is remind ourselves of the rainbows that appear afterward. It is these rainbows, these stories of hope and recovery, that can provide both comfort and inspiration to those living with BPD. These stories are not just tales; they are proof of resilience, a testament to the indomitable human spirit, and evidence that recovery, though not easy, is attainable.

Consider Elizabeth. She was diagnosed with BPD in her early twenties after years of tumultuous relationships and severe mood swings. At her lowest point, she felt like a prisoner in her own mind. But instead of succumbing to despair, she took it as a challenge. She began by educating herself about BPD, reading everything she could get her hands on. This was not just a strategy to understand her condition better but also to battle the stigma associated with it, both from society and the one she had internalized.

She sought professional help and started attending a DBT group, where she learned valuable skills such as emotional regulation and mindfulness. Elizabeth also found solace in journaling, turning her thoughts and feelings into words on a page. This not only provided a therapeutic outlet but also helped her recognize patterns in her behavior that she could work on with her therapist.

Over time, Elizabeth found her self-destructive tendencies diminishing. She felt more in control of her emotional responses, was able to maintain healthier relationships, and most importantly, started recognizing her worth. It was not an overnight transformation, and there were setbacks, but she celebrated each small victory, each step forward. Today, she is a vocal advocate for mental health awareness and uses her story to inspire others battling BPD.

What can we learn from Elizabeth's journey? It is that recovery is not a linear process. There will be moments of triumph followed by periods of struggle. Yet, each step taken, no matter how small, is a testament to your strength. And it is crucial to remember, as Elizabeth did, to acknowledge and celebrate these victories, as they are milestones on your journey toward recovery.

A story like Elizabeth's serves to remind us that while BPD is indeed a challenging disorder, it does not define who you are. It is a part of your journey, but it is not the entirety of your identity. Each person's path to recovery will be unique, but sharing these experiences builds a community of understanding and empathy. It provides solace in knowing you are not alone and that others have walked a similar path and have found their way toward recovery.

If you are dealing with BPD, draw strength from these stories. Use them as your guideposts, your beacons in the darkness. They show that with perseverance, resilience, the right tools, and support, it is possible to navigate the turbulent waters of BPD and reach a place of better mental health and peace.

Remember, your story is far from over. With every new day comes an opportunity for progress and recovery. You are more than your diagnosis, and your potential for growth and happiness is unlimited. So, even amid the glass shards of BPD, hold onto hope. It is your strongest ally, your guiding star leading you toward a brighter future.

Providing Support to Others on Their Journey With BPD

When we realize that we are not alone on our journey with BPD, the world suddenly becomes a less daunting place. That sudden moment of clarity, when everything clicks into place, can be transformative. All the emotional turbulence, the intense reactions, the fear of abandonment – they all begin to make sense when viewed through the BPD lens.

Before this understanding, many of us may have felt like an outsider, seemingly alone in our struggles. The truth, however, is far from this. BPD affects many, but sadly, a lot of us feel like we are the only ones navigating these choppy emotional waters.

My purpose in crafting this book is not only to provide you with the tools to better manage BPD but also to remind you that you are not alone on this journey. And you have the power to share this message with others who might be feeling isolated right now.

You might be wondering how. Well, it is simpler than you think and will only take a few minutes of your time.

By leaving a review of this book on Amazon, you are doing more than just sharing your feedback. You are making visible the large and supportive community that surrounds those living with BPD. Your review can guide others toward this resource that might just change their lives, as it did yours.

When you share how this book has helped you, or what new understandings it brought you, you are telling others that they are not alone. You are assuring them that there are others out there, just like them, walking the same path, facing the same struggles, and most importantly, finding ways to overcome them.

Scan to leave a review !

You are offering them a lifeline in the form of this guide without them having to do more than click a button.

Your support means more than words can express. BPD is often misunderstood, but together we can change that narrative. Thank you for joining this compassionate community and for making a difference in the lives of those living with BPD.

Chapter 7:
Navigating the BPD Labyrinth to Discover and Understand Oneself

Exploring the Intricacies of Identity Disturbance in BPD

The wilderness of our minds can be both invigorating and treacherous. A labyrinth of thoughts, beliefs, memories, and dreams. Imagine for a moment, however, that this inner wilderness is more akin to a kaleidoscope, constantly shifting, changing colors, patterns, and textures. You are not sure who you are, and the self you knew yesterday is a stranger today. This is the enigma of identity disturbance, a persistent reality for individuals with BPD.

Identity disturbance is often misunderstood. It is not just indecisiveness or occasional self-doubt; it is a chronic sense of uncertainty about oneself. Picture your self-perception as a mural, but the paints keep changing colors, the brushes switch sizes, and the canvas itself expands and contracts unpredictably. You are trying to create a self-portrait, but the image is never quite stable. That is the crux of identity disturbance.

Those living with BPD might find their self-view fluctuating. It is as though they are looking into a broken mirror, the fragments each reflecting different versions of themselves. This fragmented sense of self could lead to feelings of confusion, emptiness, and an elusive identity.

This is not about being temperamental or fickle. It is a complex struggle, akin to building a sandcastle on a windy beach, where the grains of sand are your sense of self, constantly shifting and changing.

What causes this? A mélange of factors such as genetic, environmental, and biological interplay can contribute. The echoes of childhood trauma could fracture the sense of self, leading to this splintered self-perception. Irregularities in brain regions associated with self-perception and emotional regulation could also play a significant role.

Bear in mind, though, that everyone's experience with identity disturbance is as unique as fingerprints. Some might feel a constant sense of "Who am I?" while others may grapple with fluctuations in their aspirations, values, or relationship goals.

Navigating through this maze begins with acknowledging the concept of identity disturbance. It is like stepping back from the broken mirror, and instead of focusing on each fragment, seeing it as a whole. This understanding can be the compass that guides you through the labyrinth.

Remember, patience is your ally. Creating a solid sense of self is akin to piecing together a puzzle. It takes time, reflection, and acceptance of the various facets of your identity. Every piece, even the ones that seem odd or out of place, contributes to the complete image. As the journey continues, a greater understanding of identity will surface, offering a beacon of clarity amid the ebb and flow of self-perception.

With that understanding of identity disturbance, we will explore the strategies to navigate through it in the following section. It is not an instant fix but a voyage of self-discovery and growth, revealing the wholeness that is always been within you.

Coping With Dissociation and Its Effects

If you are living with BPD, you may often encounter an unsettling sensation referred to as dissociation. Dissociation is characterized by a detachment from reality, making you feel as though you are watching life unfold from a distance, much like an outside observer rather than a participant. This might manifest as feeling disconnected from your body, experiences, and the world around you. It is as if a fog has settled between you and reality, blurring the edges and making it difficult to engage fully.

Understanding what dissociation is and why it occurs is a critical first step toward learning how to manage it. Dissociation is not a sign of weakness or failure; it is your brain's response to overwhelming situations. It is a form of self-protection, an attempt to buffer against the intensity of your feelings, whether they be anger, pain, or fear.

While it may provide temporary relief, chronic dissociation can be disruptive to your life, leading to memory gaps, difficulty focusing, and a sense of disconnection from yourself and others. It can be incredibly challenging to thrive when your reality feels distorted, so let us explore some practical strategies to navigate this territory.

Firstly, recognizing when you are experiencing dissociation is crucial. Pay attention to the signs: Feeling detached from your body, experiencing the world as unreal or dream-like, having memory lapses, or finding yourself absorbed in a fantasy world are all indicators. Be mindful of these moments without judging yourself harshly. This awareness is the first, powerful step toward grounding yourself.

Once you recognize that you are dissociating, practice grounding techniques. These strategies aim to reconnect you with the physical world, reminding you that you are here, and you are safe. One common method is the "5-4-3-2-1" grounding technique. Here is how it works: Identify five things you can see, four things you can touch, three things you can hear, two things you can smell, and one thing you can taste. This method helps you refocus your attention on your surroundings and your physical presence within them.

A similar grounding technique is mindful breathing. Sit or lie comfortably, close your eyes, and focus on your breath. Feel the air entering and leaving your body. Count your breaths if it helps to maintain focus. Try to imagine the dissociative fog lifting with each exhale, leaving clarity and presence in its wake.

Lastly, consider the role of self-care. Regular physical activity, a balanced diet, and adequate sleep can significantly impact your mental well-being, including the frequency and intensity of dissociative episodes. Consistent self-care may reduce stress levels, which can act as a trigger for dissociation.

Remember, the goal is not to eliminate dissociation completely – it is a natural response, after all. Instead, aim to manage it effectively so that it does not disrupt your life or compound your distress. Each step you take toward understanding and managing your dissociation is a step toward reclaiming control of your reality.

Remember, too, that it is okay to reach out for help. You are not alone in this journey. Mental health professionals, support groups, and trusted loved ones can provide invaluable guidance and support as you navigate the complex terrain of BPD and dissociation. Seek assistance, share your experiences, and remember, each step, no matter how small, is a step forward.

Addressing and Dealing With Self-Image Issues

We have all had that moment in front of the mirror – the time when we critically assess our reflection, sometimes with a degree of harshness that we would never dream of subjecting others to. For those living with BPD, these moments can be far more intense, an uncomfortable reality they frequently grapple with. Self-image issues can not only distort how individuals perceive themselves but also how they interact with the world around them. It is like living with an internal critic who never takes a break, constantly pointing out flaws and shortcomings that may not even exist.

Confronting this harsh inner critic is daunting, but necessary in the quest for self-understanding and acceptance. However, before we delve into practical strategies for overcoming self-image issues, let us explore why they are so common in BPD.

Firstly, understand that BPD often coexists with a disrupted sense of self-identity. This means individuals with the disorder might find it challenging to maintain a consistent, stable perception of themselves, leading to a negative or distorted self-image. Secondly, their intense emotional experiences, characteristic of BPD, can color self-perception and judgment, amplifying negative feelings about themselves.

Having clarified that, let us navigate toward some practical strategies to construct a healthier self-image. The journey is not easy, but with patience, persistence, and self-compassion, you can recalibrate the mirror you are holding up to yourself.

Counteract Negative Self-Talk: One of the initial steps is to confront the inner critic. Pay attention to your internal dialogue. When you catch yourself engaging in negative self-talk, try to counter it with positive affirmations or more balanced thoughts. This is not about deluding yourself with unrealistic positivity; instead, it is about countering disproportionately negative self-perceptions with more grounded, objective assessments.

Self-Compassion Practice: Compassion is not just for others – it is something you owe to yourself. When faced with flaws or mistakes, rather than berating yourself, practice responding with kindness and understanding. This can be as simple as speaking to yourself as you would a close friend, offering encouragement and support instead of harsh criticism.

Seek External Perspectives: Sometimes, we are our own worst critics. To balance out the possibly skewed self-perception, consider seeking external perspectives. Loved ones or trusted friends can offer a more balanced viewpoint, and therapy can provide a safe, supportive space for exploring and reconstructing self-image.

Mindfulness and Self-Acceptance: Cultivate mindfulness to stay connected with the present moment, free from judgments or assumptions. This can help you observe your thoughts without getting caught in the negativity spiral. Embrace yourself as you are now, understanding that you are a work in progress, just like everyone else.

While these are broad strategies, remember that every person's journey is unique. Tailoring these techniques to your specific situation, maybe with the help of a therapist, can make them more effective.

We have been exploring some tough terrain here, navigating the challenges of self-shame, self-judgment, and now, self-image issues. As we proceed, remember to tread gently with yourself. You are learning, and growing, and that in itself is a victory worth celebrating. In the next section, we will continue this exploration, venturing into techniques that promote self-understanding and acceptance, where we weave together the threads of self-compassion, balanced self-perception, and self-improvement.

Exploring Strategies to Foster Self-Understanding and Self-Acceptance

As you traverse through the labyrinth of your identity in BPD, each twist and turn may reveal new aspects of yourself – some welcome, others not as much. While this exploration is challenging, it is a crucial step toward healing. Understanding and accepting yourself as you are can ignite the spark of self-compassion, which is key in your recovery journey.

A significant technique for self-understanding and acceptance is self-reflection. This process involves stepping back from your emotions and thoughts and looking at them objectively. It is about asking yourself, "Why do I feel this way?" or "What triggered this reaction in me?" When you understand your responses, you can better manage your emotions, reactions, and behaviors.

Start by setting aside a quiet time for introspection each day. During this period, allow yourself to ponder the day's events, emotions, reactions, and thought patterns. A helpful tool to aid this process is journaling. Writing down your thoughts and feelings helps externalize them, making them easier to examine and understand.

Another technique is mindfulness meditation. Mindfulness is about being present in the moment, acknowledging your thoughts and feelings without judgment. This practice can improve your understanding of your emotional landscape and foster acceptance of your feelings as they come and go. Begin with short, manageable meditation sessions, gradually extending them as your comfort and familiarity with the practice grow.

When you start applying these techniques, remember to show yourself patience. Accept that there will be moments of frustration, confusion, and self-doubt. Remind yourself that self-understanding is not an overnight process – it is a journey that takes time. Instead of striving for perfection, strive for progress.

However, as you progress on this path, you might encounter facets of yourself that you find hard to accept. These are the parts of you that make mistakes, that act impulsively, that feel pain intensely. It is natural to want to reject these parts, but true self-acceptance involves acknowledging and embracing all aspects of yourself, including your flaws.

This is where self-compassion comes in. It involves treating yourself with the same kindness, understanding, and forgiveness you would show a friend. It means telling yourself, "It is okay. You are human. You make mistakes, and that is all right." This self-compassionate dialogue can help soften the harsh edges of self-criticism, providing a safe space for self-acceptance to grow.

Incorporate self-compassion exercises into your daily routine. Practice speaking to yourself kindly, especially during moments of stress or failure. Visualize embracing your flaws and mistakes, understanding they are part of your unique human journey.

Remember, while these techniques are beneficial, it is crucial to tailor them to your personal needs. What works for one person may not work for another. So, feel free to adapt these strategies or combine them with others that resonate with you.

As you venture through your journey of self-understanding and acceptance, remember, each step brings you closer to a stronger, more resilient self. It is a journey worth undertaking, not just for managing BPD, but for the profound self-growth and personal understanding that comes with it. You are more than your disorder. You are a unique individual with strengths, dreams, and the capacity for growth and healing. Embrace your journey, embrace yourself. You are worth it.

Chapter 8:
Perceiving the World in Shades of Gray

Understanding the Concept of Splitting

B orderline personality disorder is marked by a plethora of internal experiences, and among them is a distinctive phenomenon known as "splitting." Splitting is an unconscious mechanism where a person categorizes others or themselves into extremes of good or bad, lovable or detestable, reliable or unreliable – with no gray area in between. This black-and-white thinking can profoundly influence an individual's perceptions and relationships, leading to a see-saw of emotions and behaviors.

To help you understand splitting better, imagine you have a close friend who has always been there for you. But one day, they are unable to come to your aid when you need them. If you are splitting, you might suddenly view this friend as uncaring or even cruel, disregarding their past kindness. In reality, your friend might have been dealing with their own emergencies or simply made a human mistake. Still, in the throes of splitting, these nuances are hard to grasp.

The concept of splitting can seem perplexing, but it is rooted in a common human tendency to simplify complex realities. All of us, at some point, have tended to view things in a simplistic, black-and-white manner, especially during times of high stress or emotion. But in the context of BPD, this tendency is intensified and becomes a prevalent coping mechanism.

So why does splitting happen? It stems from a desire for security and consistency in an unpredictable world. Grappling with ambiguity can be emotionally taxing. Splitting, albeit unconsciously, presents a way to sidestep this discomfort by neatly categorizing people or situations into well-defined extremes. It is a survival mechanism, a way to try to control and predict the environment. But as we will see, it is a strategy that comes with significant emotional costs.

Recognizing splitting in oneself is a significant first step toward addressing it. If you notice drastic shifts in your perceptions of others or yourself, frequently swinging from idealization to devaluation, you might be experiencing splitting. But remember, self-diagnosis is not a replacement for professional help. If you recognize these patterns, it would be beneficial to reach out to a mental health professional who can provide a proper diagnosis and guide you through this.

Now, you might be asking, "Is it possible to move beyond this extreme way of thinking?" The answer is a resounding "Yes." It is essential to remember that although splitting is a complex issue, it is not a life sentence. You are not doomed to a life of emotional extremes; instead, you can move toward a more balanced, nuanced perception of the world.

As we journey further into this chapter, we will explore strategies that can help manage splitting, but before that, let us understand the impacts of this cognitive pattern in the next section, "Transcending

Extreme Thinking Patterns." As we do so, keep this image in your mind: Life is not merely black and white; it is a spectrum of shades, each one as important as the other. The world is full of complexity, and within that complexity lies immense beauty and potential for growth. It is time to start seeing in shades of gray.

Transcending Extreme Thinking Patterns

In your journey toward understanding and managing BPD, recognizing the existence of "splitting" was a significant first step. Now, let us delve into the second phase, moving beyond the realm of extreme thinking.

Understand this – when you are caught in a pattern of splitting, you might be seeing the world in binary: Good or bad, perfect or worthless, completely right or utterly wrong. This black-and-white thinking can make your life appear like a series of highs and lows, devoid of the various shades of gray that make life's tapestry richer and more meaningful.

Are you thinking, "But how do I change this? How do I escape the confining world of binary and welcome the diverse spectrum of gray?" Be reassured; the road may be challenging, but it is not impossible. Let us explore some practical strategies that can guide you through this journey.

Acknowledge Your Thoughts: Start by acknowledging the existence of your extreme thinking. Notice when you are classifying people, experiences, or things as entirely good or completely bad. Self-awareness is the foundation upon which change is built.

Practice Mindfulness: Being present in the moment can help you appreciate its complexity. When you observe your thoughts and emotions without judgment, you create a space where you can see beyond the black and white. Simple mindfulness exercises, such as focusing on your breath or observing your surroundings, can gradually train your mind to perceive subtler nuances.

Reflect on the Gray: Take a few minutes each day to think about the people and events you have categorized into extremes. Try to identify one quality or aspect that does not fit into the "all good" or "all bad" label. Remember, this does not mean you are denying the bad or downplaying the good. You are merely acknowledging the existence of a spectrum.

Question Your Thoughts: Whenever you are caught in the loop of extreme thinking, gently ask yourself, "Is there another way to see this? Am I missing out on some aspects?" Encourage your mind to consider other possibilities and perspectives.

Seek Support: Engage in discussions with trusted individuals who can offer different viewpoints. It is not about them being right and you being wrong. It is about exploring the various shades that you might have overlooked.

These practical strategies are not magic potions promising immediate transformation. They are steps toward change, and with consistency, they can help you navigate from the land of extremes to a world imbued with various hues of gray.

As you embark on this journey, remember this – it is not about discarding the black and white; it is about welcoming the gray. It is about understanding that people, experiences, and situations are complex, intricate, and multi-dimensional, just like a richly woven tapestry, full of different colors, textures, and patterns.

While these are practical steps you can begin implementing today, the following section will take you deeper into this journey. We will further explore how the extremes of love and hate can swing in BPD and provide strategies to achieve emotional balance. But for now, take a moment to breathe, appreciate your courage in taking these initial steps, and remember that you are not alone in this journey.

The Pendulum of Love and Hate

Have you ever found yourself at one end of the emotional spectrum one moment, only to swing to the other end in the next? The vast expanse of our feelings can sometimes resemble an unpredictable pendulum, swinging back and forth between extreme love and intense hatred. This rollercoaster of emotions is a hallmark of BPD, and it is particularly pronounced in the phenomenon of "splitting."

As we have discussed, splitting is a cognitive distortion where things are viewed as black or white, with no room for the shades of gray in between. It can be confusing, distressing, and exhausting to experience. However, some practical strategies and solutions can help manage these emotional extremes, fostering a sense of stability and peace.

One key strategy involves recognizing when you are in the throes of splitting. This involves developing a keen sense of self-awareness. When you feel your emotions swinging from one extreme to another, take a moment to pause. Reflect on what you are feeling. Ask yourself, "Am I viewing this situation or person as wholly good or entirely bad? Am I ignoring the complexities and nuances that actually exist?"

Journaling can be a powerful tool for increasing self-awareness. By putting your thoughts on paper, you create a tangible record of your emotions and perceptions. Over time, you may begin to see patterns in your thinking that indicate splitting. Perhaps you tend to split when you are under stress, or when you feel threatened or insecure. Recognizing these patterns is the first step toward addressing them.

Once you have identified the occurrence of splitting, you can begin to challenge this binary thinking. This process is known as cognitive restructuring, a cognitive-behavioral technique used to identify and dispute irrational or maladaptive thoughts.

One method of cognitive restructuring involves asking yourself a series of questions designed to test the validity of your black-and-white thinking. For instance, you might ask yourself, "Is there any evidence that contradicts my current view? Are there alternative explanations or viewpoints I have not considered? What are the potential consequences of thinking this way?"

Through these questions, you can begin to see the shades of gray that splitting obscures. Over time, this will help you reduce the frequency and intensity of your emotional swings, and foster a more balanced perspective.

It is essential to practice self-compassion as you work through these strategies. Remember, it is okay to feel overwhelmed sometimes. It is okay to take it slow. This journey toward emotional balance is not a race; it is a step-by-step process that requires patience, self-love, and perseverance.

The understanding and application of these tools do not happen overnight. They require practice, commitment, and time. Consider seeking professional help such as a therapist or counselor skilled in cognitive-behavioral techniques. They can guide you through this process, providing a safe and supportive environment for exploration and growth.

Remember, you are not alone in this journey. Many have walked this path before, and there is a wealth of resources and support available to you. As we move into the next section, we will dive deeper into how you can overcome the splitting trap, providing further strategies and tools to help you navigate your way to a healthier, more balanced mindset.

Escaping the Splitting Trap

Indeed, splitting, the propensity to oscillate between extremes of idealization and devaluation, can pose an intricate challenge. Yet, as with many hurdles in life, this obstacle can be overcome with persistence, resilience, and the application of new strategies.

Firstly, you might want to adopt the principle of "wise mind" from DBT. The "wise mind" is the balanced interplay between your "emotional mind" and "reasonable mind." It is the part of you that synthesizes emotional responses with logical analysis to arrive at a decision that feels right both emotionally and factually. By striving to inhabit your "wise mind," you can circumvent splitting's propensity to flip between emotional extremes.

A practical way to hone this skill is by checking the facts. When you feel an extreme emotion rising, take a moment to assess the situation. What is the factual basis for your emotion? Are there any other possible interpretations? Is your response proportional to the event? By fact-checking your emotions, you gain the upper hand and can react in a balanced way.

Secondly, consider exploring metacognitive therapy, a therapeutic approach that focuses on your thinking about thinking. This approach can be particularly effective for splitting as it encourages you to observe and reevaluate how you categorize people or situations as "all good" or "all bad." One of its exercises involves visualizing your thoughts as a train passing by, with you standing at the station. You observe each thought (or train) without necessarily getting on board. This can help foster an ability to detach from and evaluate your thoughts.

Another strategy is to embrace the power of "and." Our language often influences our thinking and vice versa. When discussing someone's qualities, for example, try using "and" instead of "but." Instead of saying, "He is caring, but he can be so selfish," try, "He is caring, and sometimes he can be selfish." This tiny linguistic shift acknowledges that multiple traits can coexist, helping you to view others in a more nuanced manner.

Last but not least, find strength in supportive communities, such as support groups for people with BPD or similar experiences. These groups are safe spaces where you can express your feelings without judgment, learn from others' experiences, and gain a sense of belonging. Sometimes, just knowing that you are not alone can make a world of difference.

Remember, change does not occur overnight, and it is all right to ask for help when you need it. Each step you take, no matter how small, is a step toward a life controlled less by splitting. Each success, no matter how minor, is a victory to be celebrated. And each setback, no matter how significant, is an opportunity to learn, grow, and become stronger.

Chapter 9:
Managing and Calming the Firestorm Within

Identifying Intense Anger in BPD

Have you ever felt a surge of anger so intense that it felt like a firestorm within you? A tumultuous tempest, so strong it threatened to consume everything in its path? Individuals dealing with BPD can often relate to these powerful and overwhelming sensations.

The first step to taming this internal storm is to understand it. As the old adage says, "Know thy enemy." Here, the "enemy" is not you or your anger, but rather, the unregulated intensity of your emotions. For individuals with BPD, anger can often be a default emotion, a fiery mask that overshadows more delicate feelings of hurt, sadness, or fear.

This kind of anger can be so intense and swift that it is often described as "zero to hundred in seconds." It may be triggered by events that others might perceive as minor or insignificant, like a casual comment, perceived criticism, or minor disagreement. But for someone with BPD, these triggers can feel like an attack, resulting in a disproportionate wave of anger.

These furious waves may feel extremely intimidating, and you might find yourself swept away by their force, but know this –

acknowledging and understanding your anger is a significant and courageous first step in learning to navigate it.

Imagine your anger as a separate entity, a physical, tangible presence. Recognizing its patterns and triggers is like learning the lay of the land, and the topography of this landscape. It is crucial to understand that the landscape is not "bad" or "negative" – it simply is. The hills, the valleys, the fiery volcanoes – they make up the terrain of your emotions. By understanding the topography, you are more equipped to navigate through it, even when the terrain is challenging.

One useful exercise could be keeping an "anger diary." Every time you experience a surge of anger, make a note of it. Write down what triggered the anger, what you were doing, who you were with, and how you reacted. Over time, you may begin to see patterns emerge, helping you to better understand your unique triggers and responses.

Understand that anger itself is not "wrong" or "bad." In many ways, it is a natural and vital human emotion, a signal that something is amiss. It can be a protective response, a shield against perceived threat or harm. The key here is not to suppress or extinguish the anger but to manage its intensity and your response to it.

Let us be clear; this is not about blaming yourself or labeling yourself as "an angry person." Far from it. It is about acknowledging that you are a person who experiences intense anger. There is a world of difference between the two. The first is an identity; the second is an experience. You are not your anger, nor are you defined by it.

As you start this journey of recognition, remember to be kind to yourself. The road to understanding and managing intense anger is not easy, and it is not a linear one. There will be setbacks and challenges, but each step you take, no matter how small, is a victory in its own right. In the next part of this chapter, we will discuss how unchecked anger can affect relationships and some strategies to manage it. But for now, give yourself credit for taking this vital first step: Recognition.

Relationships and Anger

In the quiet moments after an outburst of anger, you might find yourself puzzled, asking "How did I get here?" You are not alone in this. Anger, particularly the intense variety common in BPD, can be disorienting and disruptive, acting like a hurricane that sweeps through your life and relationships, leaving chaos in its wake.

The first step toward taming this tempest is understanding how it affects your relationships. Have you ever noticed how the atmosphere changes when you walk into a room after a display of anger? Perhaps you have seen the apprehension in the eyes of a loved one, their tension mirroring your own. The powerful energy of anger can cast long shadows over your interactions with others, even when the storm has passed.

Anger impacts relationships in several ways. First, it creates an environment of fear and unpredictability. Relationships thrive on safety and predictability, but explosive anger can shatter this sense of security. Your loved ones may begin to walk on eggshells, never knowing what might trigger your next outburst. This constant state of apprehension can lead to stress, anxiety, and even physical health issues for those in your circle.

Secondly, unchecked anger often results in hurtful words or actions that can cause lasting emotional harm. In the heat of the moment, you may say things you do not mean, causing pain that persists long after the anger has cooled. This can erode trust and intimacy, the cornerstones of any relationship, replacing them with resentment and distance.

Thirdly, your own experience of anger can impact your self-perception and how you believe others see you. Frequent episodes of intense anger can lead to feelings of guilt, shame, and worthlessness, further exacerbating feelings of isolation and loneliness.

It is crucial to remember that while anger can cause significant harm, it does not define you. Anger is an emotion, a part of your experience, but not the entirety of who you are. Your worth and value are not determined by your anger or any single emotion. This perspective shift can be the first step toward managing the impact of anger on your relationships.

So, what can you do to mitigate the effects of anger on your relationships? Firstly, communication is key. Speak with your loved ones about your experiences with anger. Help them understand that your anger is not a personal attack but rather a reflection of the emotional turmoil within you. By explaining your feelings, you invite them into your experience, fostering empathy instead of fear.

Secondly, apologize and make amends when necessary. We all say or do things we regret when we are angry. Acknowledging this and apologizing can go a long way in repairing the trust and intimacy damaged by anger. It signals to your loved ones that you recognize the impact of your behavior and are committed to change.

This is not an easy journey, but every step you take toward understanding and managing your anger is a step toward healthier, happier relationships. Remember, you are not alone in this. Countless others are walking a similar path, and there is a wealth of resources and professional help available. Together, we can learn to navigate the storm, tame the firestorm within, and reclaim the peaceful shores of our relationships.

Strategies for Managing Anger

Let us take a moment. Just inhale deeply, then exhale slowly. Feel the calming sensation that breath can bring to your stormy emotions. It is this sort of instant, practical tool that we aim to equip you with throughout this section – strategies that bring stability even amid the tumultuous sea of anger.

It is important to acknowledge that your feelings of anger are valid. You are entitled to your emotions. The key, however, lies not in suppressing these feelings, but in expressing them beneficially in your life and relationships.

Our first tool is journaling. This practice may sound old-school in our digital world, but it is a powerful method to understand, control, and navigate your emotions. Anger can cloud your judgment and warp your perspective; writing about your feelings provides clarity, offering you the distance you need to understand the source of your anger. Not only does this aid in anger management, but it also contributes to self-awareness and personal growth.

Next, we venture into cognitive restructuring, a facet of cognitive-behavioral therapy. This process aims to reshape the negative thought patterns that fuel anger. Often, during moments of anger, our thoughts become exaggerated, leading to a self-feeding cycle of escalating fury. Cognitive restructuring enables the shift from these thoughts to rational and realistic ones. For instance, instead of thinking, "Everything always goes wrong for me!" you could reframe it as, "This situation is unfortunate, but it is just a bump in the road, not the entire journey."

Thirdly, we explore progressive muscle relaxation. Anger typically carries a physical manifestation, causing muscle tension. By intentionally tensing and releasing different muscle groups, you can prompt physical relaxation, subsequently reducing the intensity of your emotions.

Communication is another potent tool in the anger management arsenal, often overlooked. It is not about arguing or shouting; it is about preventing or lessening anger outbursts through effective expression. Assertive communication revolves around voicing your feelings and needs clearly and respectfully. Instead of letting resentment build up inside, express it assertively, such as, "I feel upset when you disregard my opinion because I feel unheard."

Finally, physical exercise serves as a productive outlet for diffusing frustration and anger. It reduces the level of stress hormones in your body and triggers the release of endorphins, often termed "feel-good" hormones. From a brisk walk to an intense gym session, physical activity can help temper the fiery intensity of anger.

These tools, while straightforward, are incredibly impactful when applied consistently. However, patience and persistence are crucial, as instant relief might not always be the outcome. Remember, it is a marathon, not a sprint. As we venture into the next section, we will examine how anger's energy can be harnessed to fuel motivation and personal growth, turning setbacks into stepping stones.

Transforming Anger Into Motivation

Let me share an insight into the transformative power of fire. It is dangerous, yes, capable of destruction on a massive scale. But the fire is also a symbol of transformation and renewal. It is used to temper steel, making it stronger and more resilient. Can we apply the same principle to our anger? Let us find out.

We have talked about the destructive potential of anger in the life of someone with BPD. Now, let us pivot and look at the other side of the coin. How can we harness the energy of anger and turn it into a force for positive change? How can we convert the heat of our fury into a forge for our growth and resilience?

Consider anger as energy. In physics, energy can neither be created nor destroyed, but it can be transformed. So, how can we transform this volatile energy into something productive? How can we repurpose our raw emotions into motivation for personal development?

The first step is acceptance. Acknowledge your anger, and make peace with it. Do not suppress it or pretend it does not exist. Do not let it scare you into paralysis. Understanding the origins of your anger will help you harness its power. By recognizing and accepting your anger, you are already halfway to redirecting it.

Next, you need to understand what fuels your anger. It could be a response to a perceived injustice, a way to regain control, or a reaction to feelings of rejection or abandonment. Write these triggers down and reflect on them. This self-awareness creates an opportunity to use anger as a signal, a guidepost pointing you toward areas in your life that need attention or change.

Once you have identified these triggers, it is time to reframe your perspective. Instead of viewing these triggers as threats, see them as challenges to overcome. For instance, if rejection triggers your anger, you might feel empowered to improve your self-esteem and self-acceptance. If injustice stirs up fury, perhaps it is a sign to work toward fairness, both in your relationships and in the wider world.

By turning your triggers into targets for improvement, anger becomes a catalyst for personal growth. It pushes you out of your comfort zone, stirs you to action, and fuels your determination to change. Suddenly, your anger is not a destructive fire anymore. It is a forge, tempering you into a stronger, more resilient version of yourself.

As you channel your anger into motivation, remember to practice self-compassion. Change is a process, and it is okay to stumble along the way. It is okay to feel angry sometimes. The goal is not to eliminate anger but to transform it, to repurpose it into a force for good.

Lastly, make sure you are expressing your anger in healthy ways. Remember the strategies we have discussed for anger management? Use those. When you feel anger building, try deep breathing, mindfulness, or a brisk walk. These techniques will not just help you manage your anger, they can also give you space to think and figure out how best to channel your energy toward your goals.

Just like fire, anger is neither inherently good nor bad. Its value depends on how we use it. With the right perspective and tools, you can transform your anger into a force for personal growth and change. In the end, remember this: You are not defined by your anger, but by how you respond to it.

Chapter 10:
Creating a Network of Support

The Significance of a Robust Support Network

L ife is a journey, filled with winding paths, rocky terrains, uphill climbs, and breathtaking views. But here is the thing about journeys – they are rarely taken alone. Companionship gives us the strength to navigate the toughest terrains, support, and the courage to keep moving. Now, imagine this journey as the metaphor for managing BPD. The complex emotional landscape of BPD can seem overwhelming, but it is easier to navigate with a robust support network at your side.

A strong support network acts as the vital compass guiding you through the storm. It forms the bedrock of emotional stability and resilience, helping you bear the weight of BPD without buckling under pressure. A strong support system is not just about having people around, it is about having the right people around, those who empathize, understand, and support you in your battle with the disorder.

So, why is a robust support network so crucial when managing BPD?

First, it offers emotional anchorage. Living with BPD can often feel like being trapped in a whirlwind of intense emotions. Your support network provides an empathetic ear, an understanding heart, and compassionate words. It can be immensely therapeutic to know that you are not alone in your experiences and that others genuinely care and want to help you navigate this journey.

Second, a strong support network can act as a mirror, reflecting your feelings, thoughts, and behaviors. They provide perspective, helping you recognize harmful patterns, emotional triggers, or mood swings. With an objective, compassionate mirror to your experience, you are better equipped to understand and manage BPD symptoms.

Third, the right support system can also provide practical help. They can remind you of coping mechanisms, aid you in sticking to treatment plans, or assist in crises. Their presence can be a source of strength, a reminder of your resilience, and your capacity to manage your disorder.

Creating this network, however, is not about finding people who "fix" you. It is about surrounding yourself with individuals who believe in your strength, respect your journey, and commit to walking beside you. It is about forming connections that validate your emotions, respect your boundaries, and inspire your growth.

So, how do we create this supportive network?

Start by identifying the people in your life who exhibit understanding and compassion toward your experiences. They could be family members, friends, therapists, or members of support groups. Establish open communication with them about your struggles, your needs, and your journey. It is equally important to respect their boundaries, ensuring the relationship is mutually beneficial.

Next, consider joining BPD support groups, both offline and online. These groups consist of individuals who are going through similar experiences. They can offer unique insights, practical advice, and, most importantly, understanding without judgment.

Lastly, remember that building a strong support network is a journey in itself. It requires time, effort, patience, and constant communication. It is about fostering relationships that grow with you as you navigate the path of managing BPD.

Building this network might seem daunting, but remember, every step you take is a step toward a support system that will stand by you, helping you transform your struggle with BPD into a journey of resilience, strength, and self-discovery. As we move forward in this chapter, we will explore how to support someone with BPD and how support groups can aid in your journey.

Providing Support to Someone With BPD

As the friend, family member, or partner of someone with BPD, you play a critical role in their healing journey. It can be challenging, but your love, patience, and understanding can make a significant difference. Here is how you can support your loved one more effectively, while also taking care of your mental health.

Firstly, it is vital to educate yourself about BPD. This might seem like a given, but understanding what BPD is and how it impacts a person's thoughts, emotions, and behaviors can equip you to handle challenging situations with compassion and clarity. Remember, BPD is not a choice; it is a psychological disorder that needs professional intervention. When you comprehend the true nature of BPD, you are less likely to take things personally, and more likely to respond in ways that benefit both you and your loved one.

Secondly, maintaining open communication lines is crucial. This requires patience and active listening. At times, your loved one's words might be intense, contradictory, or even hurtful. But remember, they are grappling with overwhelming emotions they might not fully understand or control. Listen without judging, and validate their feelings even when you do not agree. This does not mean you condone harmful behavior, but it shows that you recognize their struggle and you are there for them.

When discussing sensitive topics, use "I" statements instead of "You" statements. This can help prevent the person with BPD from feeling attacked or criticized. Instead of saying, "You are overreacting," consider expressing, "I feel worried when I see you so upset over something that seems small to me." Such an approach demonstrates that you respect their emotions, even when you do not fully understand them.

Thirdly, setting clear and consistent boundaries is necessary. Supporting someone with BPD does not mean allowing them to harm you emotionally or physically. Define what is acceptable and what is not, and communicate this clearly. It is important to be consistent with these boundaries to prevent confusion or manipulation.

Alongside, learn to differentiate between supporting and enabling. While it is essential to be there for your loved one, rescuing them from every consequence of their actions can hinder their progress toward self-reliance and responsibility. Sometimes, the best support you can offer is letting them face the outcomes of their decisions while reassuring them of your love and presence.

Lastly, do not neglect your well-being. Being the primary support for someone with BPD can be draining. Make time for self-care. Reach out to support groups or seek therapy for yourself if necessary. Remember, you cannot pour from an empty cup; taking care of yourself is not selfish – it is necessary.

In the end, remember that progress may be slow, and setbacks are part of the process. Yet, your consistent support, tempered with respect for your well-being, can make a significant difference in your loved one's journey toward managing BPD. It can also deepen your relationship, building bridges of understanding and empathy that stand the test of time.

Engaging With Support Groups and Communities

The journey of living with or caring for someone with BPD can often feel like a lonely one, like sailing in uncharted waters with no land in sight. However, rest assured that you are not alone. There are myriad support groups and communities available, ready to lend an ear, share their experiences, or offer valuable advice. Such platforms provide safe spaces for people to express their feelings, share their struggles, and learn from others who are in the same boat. So, how does one go about finding these invaluable resources?

To start, mental health organizations and hospitals often have links with local support groups and can provide information about them. Reach out to such organizations in your area, inquire about the support groups they are aware of, and request to be connected. You could also use online search engines to find local and national groups that cater to individuals dealing with BPD or their caregivers. However, ensure that you verify their credibility before getting involved.

Online platforms, in particular, have revolutionized the accessibility and convenience of support groups. These virtual communities can be a lifeline for those who live in remote areas, those with mobility issues, or even those who just prefer the comfort and privacy of their homes. Websites and apps such as Meetup, Facebook, and Reddit have numerous groups dedicated to BPD discussions. The beauty of these platforms lies in their ability to cater to niche needs. For instance, you might find a group specifically for parents caring for children with BPD, or one for spouses of individuals diagnosed with BPD.

When choosing a group, whether online or offline, there are a few considerations to keep in mind. Firstly, make sure the group's meeting times fit within your schedule. Second, ensure the group's ethos aligns with your needs. For instance, some groups may have a more educational focus, offering sessions with experts, while others might lean more toward open discussions among members. It is important to find a group where you feel comfortable and supported.

Participating in these support groups offers a myriad of benefits. By sharing experiences and coping strategies, group members can empower each other, reduce feelings of isolation, and increase their understanding of the disorder. However, remember that while these support groups provide tremendous help, they are not a replacement for professional help and should be used as a complementary resource.

Getting involved in a community does not mean you have to share your story right away, or at all. It is perfectly okay to attend meetings or observe online discussions without actively participating until you feel ready to do so. Similarly, if you join a group and realize it is not the right fit for you, do not hesitate to look for another one. The aim is to find a safe space where you feel understood, heard, and accepted.

Lastly, remember that everyone's journey with BPD is unique. While hearing others' experiences can provide insight and reassurance, it is essential to remember that what worked for one person might not work for another. Hence, take the advice given in support groups with a grain of salt and always consult with a mental health professional for personalized advice.

As you tread the often-challenging path of BPD, remember, "Many hands make light work." The right community or support group can help carry the load, making the journey significantly more manageable.

The Vital Role of Family and Friends in the Recovery Process

The journey of managing BPD is often a tumultuous one, filled with a series of emotional crests and troughs. Having supportive family and friends throughout this journey can make a world of difference, helping to bring solace amid the storm. But what does this support look like, and how can it be provided most effectively? Let us dive deeper into understanding this essential aspect of recovery.

Being a companion to someone battling BPD is akin to walking a tightrope. On one end, you have the natural urge to envelop your loved one in understanding, compassion, and acceptance. On the other, you need to draw boundaries for self-preservation. This balancing act is vital, but it is equally important to know that you are a pillar of strength, not a solution to the problem.

First and foremost, education is crucial. Understanding BPD, its triggers, the emotional rollercoaster, and the coping mechanisms can equip you with the right tools to offer appropriate support. This understanding can also help to dispel any misconceptions, fostering empathy and patience in dealing with difficult situations.

Next, effective communication is the cornerstone of support. Your loved one is likely to experience intense emotions, self-shaming, and mood swings. Hence, being open, honest, and non-judgmental in your communication can make them feel heard and validated. Practicing active listening, validating their feelings without endorsing their self-destructive behavior, and maintaining a calm demeanor even in the face of emotional outbursts can be incredibly beneficial.

Furthermore, encourage and promote professional help. Remind them of the benefits of therapeutic interventions and medications, and if possible, offer to accompany them for appointments. The reassurance that they do not have to navigate these daunting steps alone can be a powerful motivator.

Additionally, during times of crisis, your presence can be the buoy that keeps them afloat. Learning about crisis management strategies can help you recognize warning signs of self-harm or suicidal ideation and act appropriately. It is important to know when to reach out to professionals and ensure that the individual is not left alone during these critical times.

But, amid all this, it is also essential to practice self-care. It can be challenging and emotionally draining to support someone with BPD. Set boundaries to ensure you are not being pulled under in the process of trying to keep someone else afloat. Your well-being is equally important. Do not shy away from seeking help for yourself, be it professional counseling or joining a support group for families and friends of individuals with BPD.

Remember, you are an ally, a beacon of hope, and a pillar of strength. Your role is not to fix them, but to stand by them, providing stability in their world of emotional turbulence. Your companionship can help them rediscover their worth, learn to manage their emotions and live a fulfilling life despite their diagnosis. Your love, understanding, and resilience can help foster their healing, one step at a time.

So, while the journey might be challenging, it can also be deeply rewarding. By offering your support, you are not just helping your loved one manage BPD; you are also fostering a relationship based on mutual respect, empathy, and unconditional love.

Chapter 11:
Setting Forth on the Path of Healing

Effective and Scientifically Proven Treatments

Y ou are not alone. If you or someone you care about is struggling with BPD, please remember this. It can be a challenging condition, often causing intense emotional highs and lows, an unstable sense of self, and difficulties with interpersonal relationships. But there is hope. With the appropriate treatments and support, living a meaningful and fulfilling life is entirely within your reach.

Imagine a toolshed. It is filled with various implements, each designed to serve a specific purpose. The gardener does not use the same tool for all tasks; he selects the right one based on the job at hand. Similarly, mental health professionals have a metaphorical toolshed filled with evidence-based treatments that are scientifically validated for effectiveness.

When it comes to BPD, several such therapies have proven particularly effective. You might think of these therapies as the gardener's go-to tools – those reliable implements that get pulled out time and time again because they are the best fit for the job.

The top three treatments that we will discuss are dialectical behavior therapy (DBT), cognitive behavioral therapy (CBT), and pharmacological interventions, or simply put, medication. Further down the line, we will also look at eye movement desensitization and reprocessing (EMDR).

Now, let us begin with a brief overview of these three main treatments.

Dialectical behavior therapy, developed by psychologist Marsha M. Linehan in the late 1980s, was the first therapy proven effective for BPD. It combines traditional cognitive-behavioral techniques with concepts of mindfulness, acceptance, and change. It helps individuals to regulate emotions, control self-destructive behaviors, and improve relationships – core struggles in BPD. This therapy emphasizes balance and encourages patients to accept their experiences while simultaneously working toward change.

Next, we have cognitive behavioral therapy. Although not specifically designed for BPD like DBT, CBT has shown effectiveness in treating the condition. It operates on the belief that our thoughts affect our feelings and behaviors. In other words, change your thoughts, and you change your world. This technique teaches individuals with BPD to identify negative thought patterns, challenge them, and replace them with healthier ones.

Finally, medication. While no drugs are FDA-approved specifically for BPD, certain types of medication – like antidepressants, mood stabilizers, and antipsychotics – can help manage particular symptoms or co-occurring conditions. It is important to remember that medication is not a stand-alone solution but is often used in conjunction with therapies like DBT and CBT.

In the sections to follow, we will dive deeper into each of these treatments, unpacking how they work, their benefits, and how they can be tailored to meet individual needs. But before we move on, take a moment to reflect. How do you feel about these therapies? Do any of them resonate with you more than others? Remember, you are not just a passive recipient in your healing journey – you are an active participant. Your perspective matters. It is okay to have questions, concerns, or even skepticism. That is part of the process, part of your path toward healing.

Delving Into the Realms of DBT, CBT, and EMDR

Imagine, if you will, standing at the entrance of a garden maze. The hedges rise high above your head, obscuring what lies ahead. You know there is a path to the center, but which way to go? The labyrinth of mental health treatments can often feel the same. Daunting, complex, and overwhelming. But fear not, for just like in that maze, there are guides and signposts to help navigate you on your journey. Let us delve into three such signposts –DBT, CBT, and EMDR.

Marsha Linehan, a psychologist, initially developed DBT to treat people with BPD. It works by combining standard cognitive-behavioral techniques for emotional regulation with concepts of distress tolerance and acceptance derived from Zen Buddhism. This balanced approach gives DBT its name, embodying the dialectic or balance between acceptance and change.

Consider it like this, you are on a tightrope, trying to cross a chasm. On one side, there is acceptance, acknowledging your feelings and experiences without judgment. On the other, there is change, the active steps you can take to modify your behavior. This technique acts as your balancing pole, helping you traverse the line between these two aspects to arrive at a healthier state of mind.

On to CBT, which stands as one of the most widely utilized forms of therapy for a variety of mental health conditions, including BPD. It focuses on identifying and addressing maladaptive thoughts and behaviors. Picture your mind as a garden. Negative thoughts are the weeds that overrun and choke your positive blooms. This approach provides you with the necessary tools – a cognitive hoe, if you will – to uproot those weeds and nurture healthier thinking patterns.

Now, EMDR, although less known than DBT and CBT, has shown promise for BPD, particularly when traumatic experiences underlie the disorder. This technique works by helping you process and integrate distressing memories, thereby reducing their emotional impact. It is akin to cleaning a dirty window pane. The memories, like the pane, do not disappear, but EMDR helps clear the grime, allowing a less distressing view of the past.

Despite the effectiveness of these therapies, it is crucial to remember that each person's experience with BPD is unique. There is no one-size-fits-all approach. You may find one therapy resonates more than another, or you might benefit from a blend of all three. And that is perfectly okay.

Ultimately, your journey through the maze of BPD is your own. With the guidance of skilled therapists and these therapeutic approaches, you have the map to navigate toward the center, toward your healing. It may not be an easy journey, but it is one filled with growth, self-discovery, and resilience.

Keep in mind that these therapies do not provide a quick fix, but rather equip you with lifelong skills to manage your emotions, handle distress, and develop healthier relationships.

In our next stage of exploration, we will consider other paths that can also contribute to this journey – complementary and holistic therapies. They may not replace these therapies but can certainly enhance the overall healing process. But for now, let the concepts of DBT, CBT, and EMDR sink in. Reflect on them, read about them, and discuss them with your therapist if you have one. Remember, understanding is the first step to healing.

Exploring Complementary and Holistic Therapies

Imagine strolling through a lush forest, each breath filled with the scent of dew-kissed leaves. Your footsteps rhythmically sync with the heartbeat of the earth. This serenity, this sense of oneness with the world around us, is not just a metaphor but also a glimpse into the power of holistic therapies. In the journey toward healing from BPD, we will explore these complementary approaches, aiming to synergize them with our primary treatments like DBT, CBT, and EMDR.

Holistic therapies consider the entire person: Mind, body, and spirit. It is like weaving a strong rope from separate strands – our physical health, our thoughts and emotions, and our connection to the world around us. This interconnectivity forms the cornerstone of therapies like mindfulness, yoga, and art therapy, which could potentially bolster our healing journey.

Picture this: You are sitting comfortably, your eyes closed. There is no aim, no goal, just you and your breath. This is mindfulness, the art of being present. For people with BPD, the mind is often a tempest of emotions and thoughts. Mindfulness is like an anchor in this storm, grounding you in the here and now. It can be as simple as observing your breath, noticing the sensation of air entering and leaving your body. Over time, mindfulness can help you become more aware of your emotional state, making it easier to manage intense feelings and reduce impulsive behaviors, common in BPD.

Now, let us talk about the ancient practice of yoga. It is not just about twisting your body into pretzel-like poses. Yoga fosters a profound mind-body connection. The slow, deliberate movements coupled with conscious breathing can help soothe the emotional turbulence often experienced by those with BPD. A study published in "Evidence-Based Complementary and Alternative Medicine" suggested yoga could reduce impulsivity and mood instability, key characteristics of BPD. Start with gentle yoga styles like Hatha or Restorative yoga, and remember: It is not about perfect poses, but the process of tuning into your body and breaths.

Finally, let us delve into the colorful world of art therapy. Art can be a non-verbal language, a medium to express what is hard to put into words. An empty canvas becomes a safe space to project your emotions. The act of creating art can be therapeutic, allowing for emotional catharsis. For individuals with BPD, who often struggle with self-image and identity issues, art therapy can provide a mirror to self-reflect and explore various facets of their identity.

Of course, it is essential to remember these are complementary therapies. They do not replace but augment evidence-based treatments like DBT and CBT. Everyone's journey is unique, and what works for one may not work for another. It is about experimenting, being open to new experiences, and finding what resonates with you.

Each of these therapies offers a unique path toward healing. Mindfulness anchors us in the present, yoga unifies mind and body, and art therapy allows for emotional expression. As we stitch these strands together, we weave our strong rope to aid in our climb toward recovery from BPD.

Your journey may begin with a single mindful breath, a simple yoga pose, or a stroke of color on canvas. And in these moments, you are not just a person with BPD; you are a mindful observer, a yogi, an artist – reaching out to the world in your unique way, navigating your healing journey.

Customizing Treatment to Suit Personal Needs and Circumstances

In the journey to healing from BPD, we have spoken about various treatment methods and therapeutic techniques. However, it is essential to underline the importance of tailoring these treatments to suit your unique needs and circumstances. There is no one-size-fits-all approach to mental health care, and what works for one person may not work for another. The crucial factor is the acknowledgment of your individuality and the respect for your unique experience with BPD.

To begin, it is essential to understand your own mental health landscape. This requires introspection and may often involve a licensed mental health professional who can guide you through this process. Take time to understand your triggers, your emotional responses, your coping mechanisms, and your patterns of behavior. Each person's experience with BPD is colored by a multitude of factors, including their life experiences, their physical health, their personal relationships, and their emotional resilience. By understanding your unique perspective, you can better tailor your treatment plan to effectively manage your BPD.

Another crucial aspect of tailoring treatment to personal needs is open communication with your healthcare provider. In this regard, do not be shy to voice out your concerns and your feelings. If a particular method makes you uncomfortable, express it. If another strategy has proven effective for you in the past, bring it up. Your therapist or counselor is there to guide you, and their guidance will be more effective if they fully understand your experience. They are your ally in this journey, and your insights are crucial to crafting a personalized treatment plan.

Practicing self-compassion is another aspect of tailoring treatment to personal needs. It is easy to get caught up in the whirlwind of trying to "fix" ourselves that we forget to be kind to ourselves. Remember, healing is not about eradicating every flaw. It is about learning to live with our flaws and turning them into strengths. Self-compassion encourages us to view our struggles as part of our shared human experience, encouraging us to be kind to ourselves during the healing process. You are more than your disorder, and acknowledging this is a fundamental part of the healing journey.

Finally, remember that healing is not a race. Progress can sometimes be slow, and that is okay. There will be good days and bad days, but what matters is that you keep moving forward. Celebrate your victories, no matter how small they seem. Each step you take toward your well-being is a step worth celebrating.

In the end, treatment is not about curing BPD overnight but about managing its symptoms, minimizing its impact on your life, and improving your overall quality of life. And the most effective treatment is the one that respects your unique journey and supports you in the way that you need. Keep in mind that it is your journey, your healing, and ultimately, your life. Personalizing your treatment strategy will ensure that you remain at the center of this process, reminding you that you are in control.

Chapter 12:
Embarking on the Path Ahead

Setting Realistic Recovery Expectations

A s dawn breaks, promising a fresh start, let us take a deep breath and prepare to embark on this journey together – a journey of recovery. For some of you, the path may seem daunting. Rest assured, though, that it is not a sprint, but a marathon. Recovery from BPD is a long-term commitment, and it is crucial to set realistic expectations as we navigate this path.

Let us first acknowledge that recovery does not mean "curing" BPD or eradicating its existence. That is a common myth and an unrealistic goal that could lead to disappointment. Instead, recovery means learning to manage symptoms, fostering resilience, and improving your overall quality of life. It is about regaining control over your emotions, developing healthier relationships, and discovering your authentic self amid the chaos that BPD often brings.

At this point, you might ask, "How long will it take me to recover?" The answer is as unique as each individual reading these lines. Recovery is not a one-size-fits-all process. It varies from person to person, depending on multiple factors such as your unique BPD symptoms, personal resilience, support network, and how consistently you engage with your treatment plan. The key here is to embrace patience, understanding that it is not about the speed but the direction.

Imagine your recovery journey as a beautiful piece of art. Just as an artist does not rush the process but appreciates each stroke of the brush, each color mix, and each textural change, similarly, your journey requires time and patience. Every small step, every moment of self-realization, every instance of emotional control, and every improvement in your relationships is a victory. Cherish them.

Moreover, it is important to understand that your journey may not be linear. It is common to experience setbacks along the way, days where you might feel like you have taken two steps back. This is a normal part of the recovery process. Instead of viewing these instances as failures, try to see them as learning opportunities. What triggered your setback? What coping strategies did you try? Could you approach the situation differently next time? Remember, you are not back at square one with each setback, but rather, it is a winding path up a mountain – you are still making progress, even when it does not feel like it.

Moreover, be gentle with yourself as you navigate this road. Hold yourself accountable, but also offer yourself grace and compassion. Celebrate your small victories – they are the building blocks of your larger success story. And most importantly, remind yourself why you embarked on this journey in the first place. Your "why" is your guiding star – it will keep you motivated when the journey feels challenging.

Setting realistic expectations does not mean setting the bar low. It means acknowledging that recovery is a process. It means understanding that it is okay not to be okay sometimes. It means knowing that every step you take, no matter how small, is a step toward a better future.

The healing journey for BPD is not a neatly paved, straight path, but a winding trail through a thick forest. It requires endurance, patience, and determination. There will be challenges and obstacles along the way, but with realistic expectations, you can navigate this trail with resilience and grace, basking in the beauty of your progress, and savoring the richness of the journey.

Inspiring Stories of Triumph and Recovery

A journey with BPD can be harrowing, arduous, and often lonely, filled with storms that seem to upend the sea of one's emotions. But it is essential to remember that amid the tumultuous waves, there also exist islands of hope and resilience. It is these stories of triumph and recovery that offer the glimmer of a sunrise after a long, challenging night.

Take Jane, for example. She was diagnosed with BPD in her early twenties after a tumultuous period filled with mood swings, impulsive decisions, and intense fear of abandonment. Jane's life was in disarray; she felt lost in a labyrinth of her mind, unable to find an exit. However, her diagnosis was not a life sentence but the beginning of her healing journey.

For Jane, recovery did not mean the absence of BPD symptoms but learning how to manage them effectively. She began attending therapy, where she learned to identify her triggers, manage her mood swings, and employ mindfulness to stay in the present. Jane also learned the importance of setting boundaries in relationships, reducing her fear of abandonment. She began to see her condition not as a barrier but as a part of her that required understanding and care.

Through the years, Jane's life saw significant improvement. The rocky path she once tread became smoother as she took control of her emotional responses. She started mending her relationships and even took up painting, using her creativity as an outlet for her intense emotions. Jane began to see that her life, though fraught with challenges, was also filled with triumphs, large and small. Her journey with BPD became a testament to resilience and a beacon of hope for others navigating similar paths.

We can also look at Robert's story. Diagnosed with BPD in his late twenties, Robert often experienced intense bouts of anger, a common symptom of BPD. This anger negatively affected his relationships and work life. The diagnosis was an eye-opener for Robert, who realized the need to seek help.

Robert decided to attend therapy, specifically DBT, which was particularly effective for individuals with BPD. Through this, he learned to recognize his anger triggers and develop coping mechanisms, such as deep breathing and mindfulness exercises.

Over time, Robert was able to tame his inner firestorm. His relationships improved, and he was better able to manage his emotions at work. His story became another testament to the fact that while BPD poses challenges, recovery, management, and the ability to lead a fulfilling life are well within reach.

Stories like Jane's and Robert's serve as reminders that recovery, while a difficult and personal journey, is indeed possible. They are living testaments to the potential within each person diagnosed with BPD. Their stories provide not only hope but also practical examples of how to manage the disorder.

Remember, each person's journey is unique, and recovery does not look the same for everyone. It is about finding balance, understanding yourself, and learning to navigate the complexities of your emotions. Be patient with yourself as you embark on this journey. As these stories demonstrate, with perseverance and the right tools and support, you can certainly pave your path to recovery.

Building a Repertoire of Effective Coping Skills and Self-Care Practices

Are you familiar with the popular adage, "You cannot pour from an empty cup?" This saying has lingered throughout the years due to its profound wisdom. If we do not take care of ourselves first, we simply cannot take care of others effectively, let alone handle our daily responsibilities.

Self-care has become a bit of a buzzword in recent times and for good reason. This is particularly true for those dealing with mental health issues like BPD. Self-care is not just about spa days or treating yourself to a dessert, it is about taking holistic care of your physical, mental, and emotional health. Now, let us explore how you can cultivate effective coping skills and self-care practices that will empower you in your journey with BPD.

Physical self-care involves activities that improve your physical health, such as regular exercise, balanced nutrition, adequate sleep, and regular medical checkups. Physical health is directly connected to mental health; maintaining a routine that promotes physical well-being can help manage BPD symptoms. Exercise, for instance, releases endorphins, known as "feel-good" hormones, that can elevate mood and act as natural anti-depressants. Choose a form of physical activity that you enjoy – it could be as simple as walking, yoga, or dancing. Make it a part of your daily routine.

Next, let us talk about mental self-care. It is crucial to engage in activities that stimulate your mind and help reduce stress. This could be reading, writing, solving puzzles, painting – whatever works best for you. These activities can provide a healthy escape and help maintain cognitive function. It is also important to practice mindfulness. Whether it is through meditation or just sitting quietly with your thoughts, mindfulness can help you stay grounded and focused.

Emotional self-care is all about recognizing and respecting your feelings. BPD can often lead to emotional turbulence; taking time to process these emotions is crucial. Journaling can be a potent tool for this purpose – it allows you to express your feelings without judgment, which can be therapeutic. Furthermore, learning to say "No" when things get overwhelming is a part of emotional self-care. It is okay to put your well-being first.

Finally, social self-care involves nurturing relationships that make you feel loved and supported. Surround yourself with people who understand your struggles and offer a safe space for expression. Joining support groups can also provide a sense of community and shared understanding. It is also okay to step away from toxic or draining relationships.

Remember that self-care is deeply personal and what works for one person may not work for another. It is essential to find practices that you genuinely enjoy and that are easy to incorporate into your routine. Over time, these practices can become second nature, equipping you with the tools to manage stress, navigate emotional storms, and embrace life more fully.

In a nutshell, prioritizing self-care is not a luxury – it is a necessity. In the grand journey of healing and recovery from BPD, do not forget that it is not selfish to put yourself first. It is through tending to your own needs that you gather the strength to face the challenges that come your way. As we move to the next section, we will see how hope and resilience, the twin beacons of recovery, can be kindled and nurtured over time.

Embracing Hope and Cultivating Resilience in BPD

As you traverse this complicated journey through the landscape of BPD, it is vital to remember one fundamental aspect: You are resilient, and there is hope. It may sometimes seem like an elusive concept, particularly in times of distress, but hope is the beacon that will guide you through your darkest hours. It is the wind in your sails, the catalyst for change, and the driving force behind your will to push forward.

To embrace hope, start by setting small, achievable goals for yourself. Maybe today you managed to resist a self-destructive urge or practiced mindfulness when emotions were raging. Celebrate these victories, however small they may seem. They are stepping stones on your path to recovery.

Remember, it is not about comparing your progress to others. Everyone's journey is unique and unfolds at their own pace. What matters is that you are moving forward, even if it is just one small step at a time. The journey of a thousand miles begins with a single step, and your first step is to acknowledge and appreciate the progress you are making.

Now, let us talk about resilience. It is not just about the ability to bounce back from adversity. It is about learning, growing, and transforming the ashes of struggle into fertile soil for future growth. You have already shown resilience by choosing to embark on this journey, by choosing to fight, and by choosing to seek help.

Building resilience is a lifelong process, but there are some practices you can incorporate into your daily life to nurture this quality. Regular mindfulness exercises, like meditation and yoga, can help foster resilience by promoting a sense of calm and helping you manage stress. Building and maintaining healthy relationships also contribute to resilience, offering emotional support when needed.

Learn to express your emotions healthily, whether that is through writing, talking to someone you trust, or engaging in creative outlets like painting or playing an instrument. It can help in processing your feelings, reduce the intensity of your emotional reactions, and provide a sense of relief.

Engage in physical activity regularly. It might be a walk in the park, a gym workout, or dancing to your favorite music. Physical activity not only boosts your mood and reduces stress but also fosters resilience by making you feel strong and capable.

Cultivating a growth mindset can significantly contribute to resilience. Embrace challenges as opportunities for learning, view failures as temporary setbacks, and see effort as the pathway to mastery. Believing in your ability to improve and adapt is a powerful ally in your journey toward recovery.

Importantly, be patient with yourself. Building resilience takes time, and there will be setbacks. But remember, it is not about how many times you fall; it is about how many times you get back up. As the Japanese proverb says, "Fall seven times, stand up eight."

Embrace self-compassion. Treat yourself with the same kindness and understanding you would give to a friend in a similar situation. Acknowledge your feelings without judgment, recognize that everyone makes mistakes and struggles, and remember to take care of yourself.

Amid the storm that BPD might sometimes seem, remember that resilience is not just about weathering it but learning how to dance in the rain. Hold onto hope, for it is the promise of a brighter tomorrow, the affirmation that the current hardships are temporary, and the assurance that you are stronger than your struggles.

Passing the Baton Forward

Dear reader,

I am deeply grateful that you chose to journey through my book. I hope that the content has provided valuable insight and helped in cultivating a better understanding of borderline personality disorder.

As you begin applying these strategies and insights to navigate life's challenges, you might wonder how impactful it would have been to possess this knowledge earlier. While time travel remains an elusive concept, there is a way you can assist others in their journey – by sharing your candid opinion of this book on Amazon.

Scan to leave a review !

Your authentic review can serve as a guiding light for others who are in search of information and strategies for managing BPD and nurturing healthier relationships. As an independent author, your feedback not only helps improve my work but significantly impacts the visibility of the book, enabling it to reach a wider audience.

If you could spare a moment to write a review on Amazon, it would mean a great deal to me. I assure you; I will read it personally.

All feedback, whether it reflects positive experiences or areas for improvement, is deeply appreciated.

Thank you for your time, and I eagerly look forward to reading your thoughts.

Sincerely,

Lois Frost

Final Words

As we draw to the close of this journey, it is important to recognize that the key to thriving with borderline personality disorder lies in the understanding and implementation of the strategies that have been shared. We have delved into the core of BPD, demystifying its complexities, and illuminating the paths toward safeguarding your mental health and fostering healthier relationships.

Remember, living with BPD does not define you, rather it is an aspect of your life that you can manage effectively. The life-changing tools provided in this book aim to empower you in that journey, strengthening your resilience and opening the door to a life of balance and fulfillment.

You are not alone on this journey. Many have walked this path before you, and many will walk it after. The courage to face the challenges and the commitment to apply these strategies to your life will lead to profound changes. Embrace the wisdom found within these pages and in doing so, allow yourself the space for growth and transformation.

Now, I implore you to apply these insights to your life. Incorporate these strategies into your daily routines. Observe the changes, however subtle they may be initially, and celebrate your victories, no matter how small. It is in these small steps that significant transformations take root.

Before we part ways, allow me to share a personal note. Your journey may be challenging, and there may be days when the road ahead seems daunting, but remember, resilience is forged in the crucible of trials. Never lose sight of your inner strength and never underestimate your ability to overcome.

Good luck on your journey, dear reader. Embrace it with courage, persist with determination, and remember to be kind to yourself. This journey is yours, and every step you take toward understanding and managing your BPD is a step toward a life of greater peace, fulfillment, and positive relationships. Let this book be your guide and your solace, a beacon of light in moments of doubt, and a reminder of the powerful being that you are.

About the Author

A storyteller at heart, Lois Frost weaves a rich tapestry of human emotions, triumphs, and struggles in her writing. Her unique perspective on psychology, human relationships, and the complexities of the human mind allows her to create content that resonates deeply with her readers and facilitates their journey toward understanding and self-improvement.

The inspiration for Lois's writing was born out of her fascination with the intricacies of human behavior. An avid reader from a young age, Lois was drawn to narratives that focused on the human psyche, eventually sparking her own journey into writing, a journey characterized by deep introspection and emotional honesty.

Lois's gift for creating a strong bond between her readers and her narrative stems from her own experiences and her innate ability to empathize with diverse perspectives. She believes in the transformative power of empathy and introspection, and through her writings, she strives to help her readers develop understanding, acceptance, and compassion.

Despite the depth and seriousness of her work, Lois maintains a light-hearted approach to life. She strongly believes in the healing power of laughter and seeks joy in the simple pleasures of life. When not weaving narratives, Lois indulges in her love for comedy and amateur theatre. She also enjoys hiking, playing the piano, and stargazing, often drawing inspiration from these experiences for her creative work.

In essence, Lois Frost is a beacon of compassion and wisdom, guiding her readers on their journey to better understand themselves and others. Her work stands as a testament to her belief that literature has the power to touch lives, heal wounds, and encourage a profound exploration of the human psyche.

www.ingramcontent.com/pod-product-compliance
Lightning Source LLC
Chambersburg PA
CBHW071134280326
41935CB00010B/1225